Your first and last name:

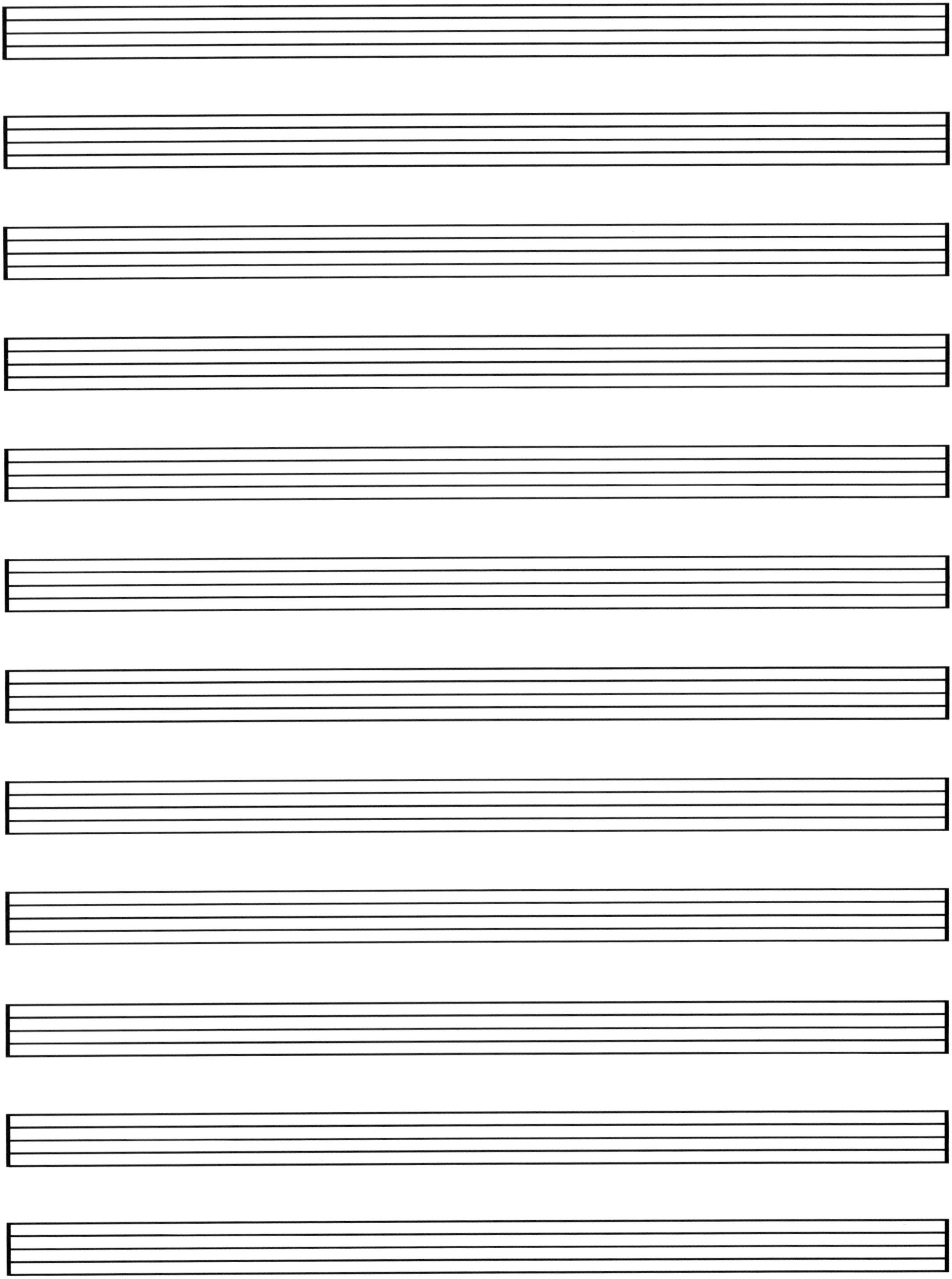

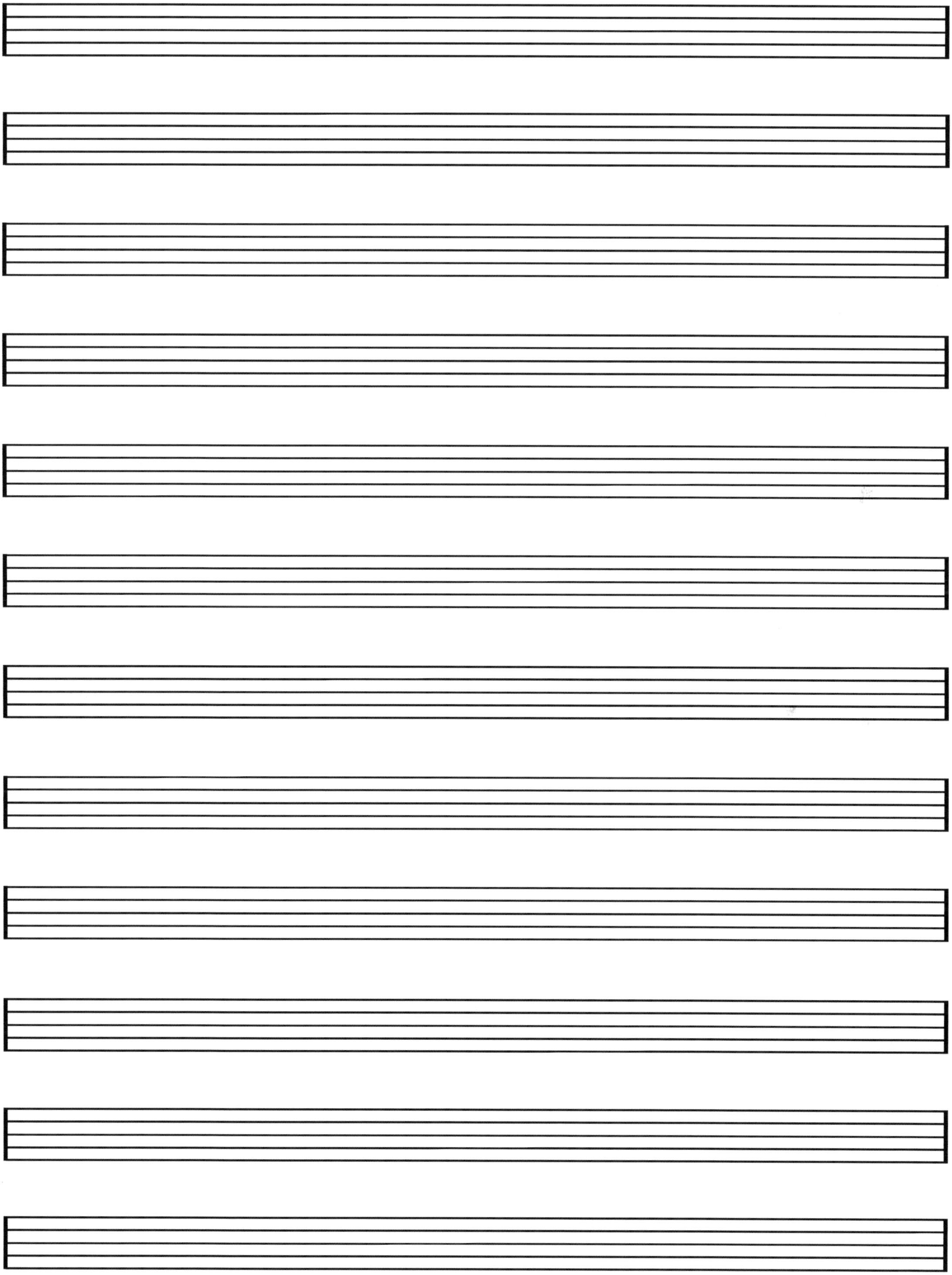

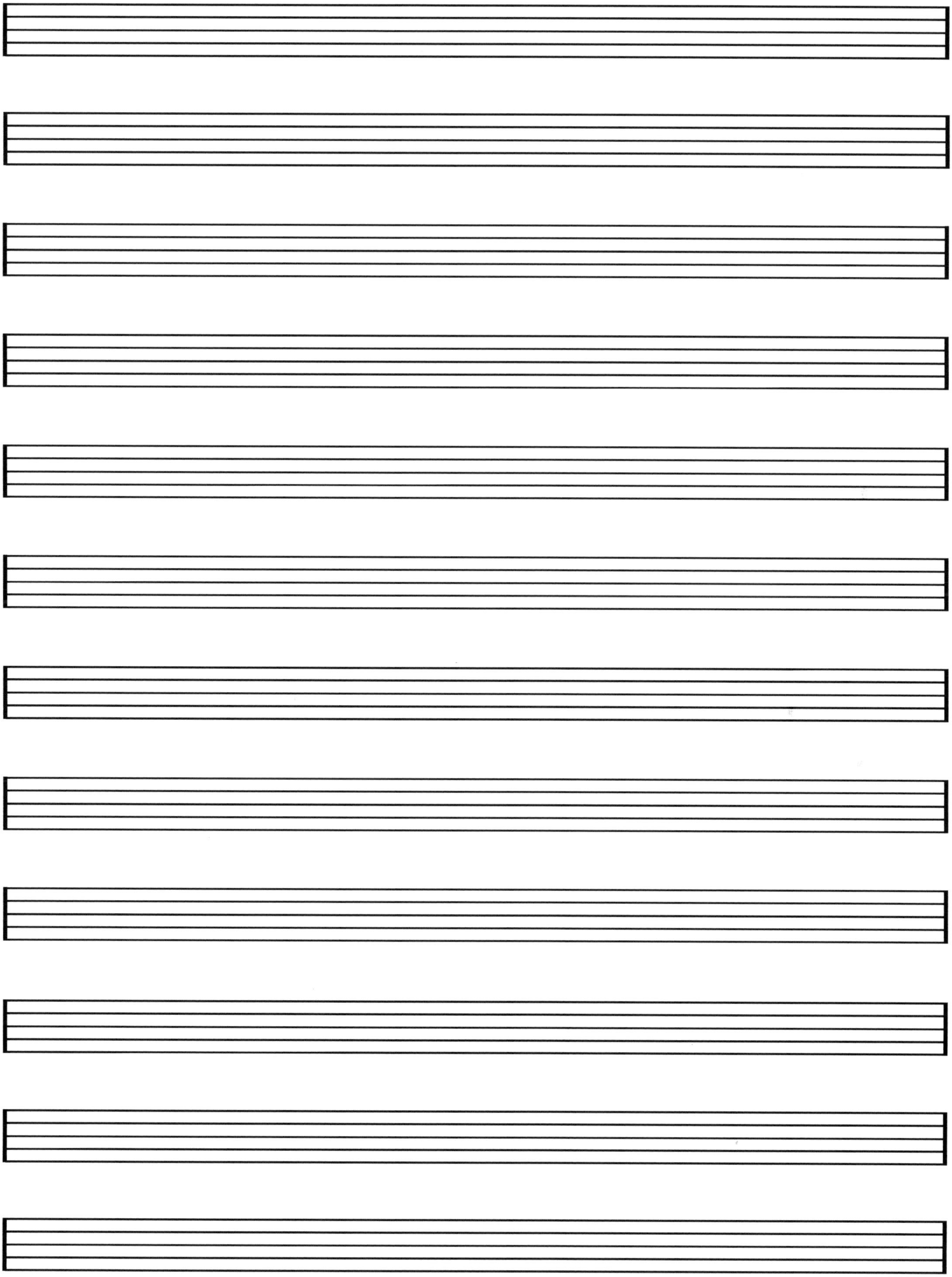

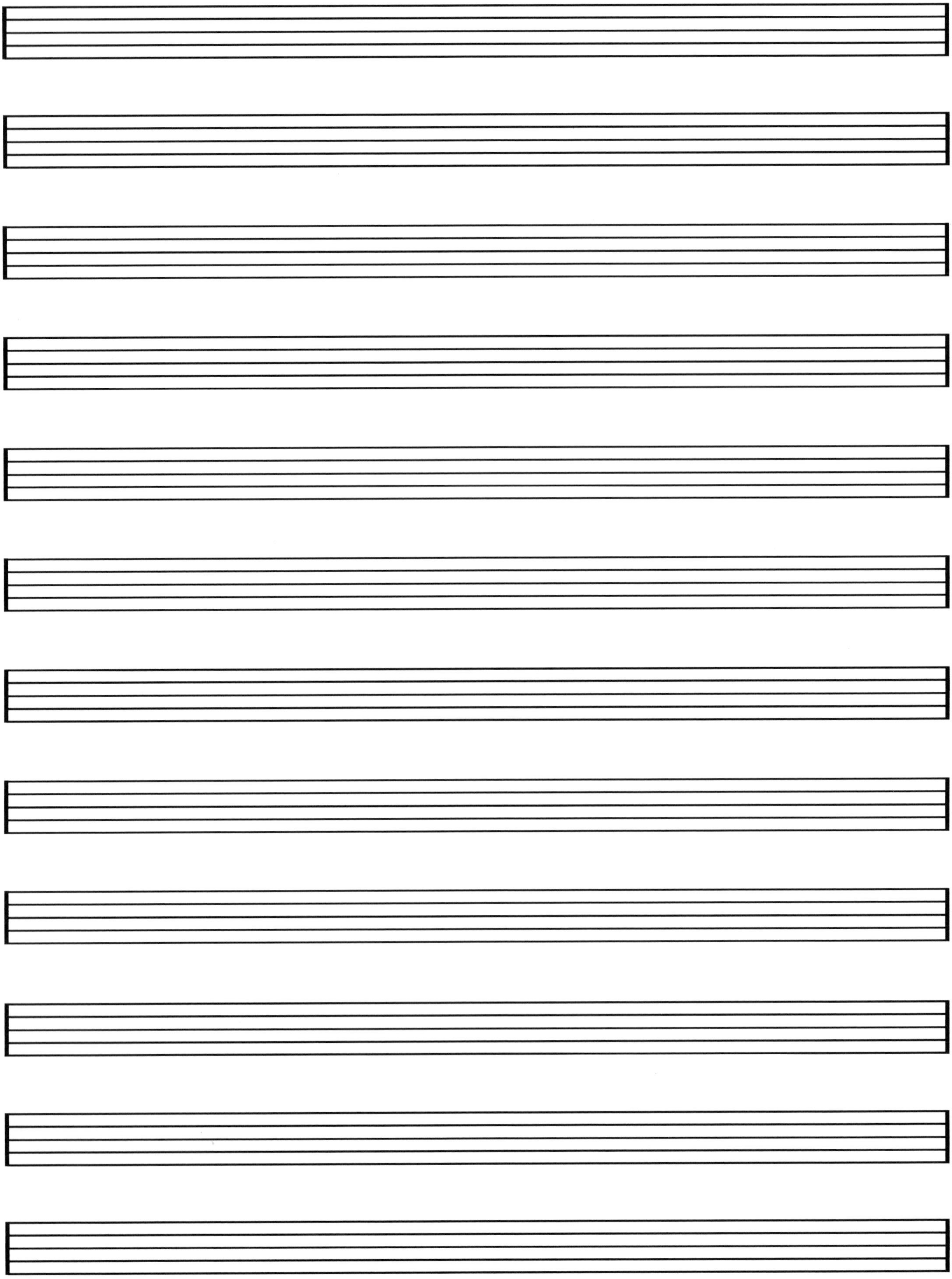

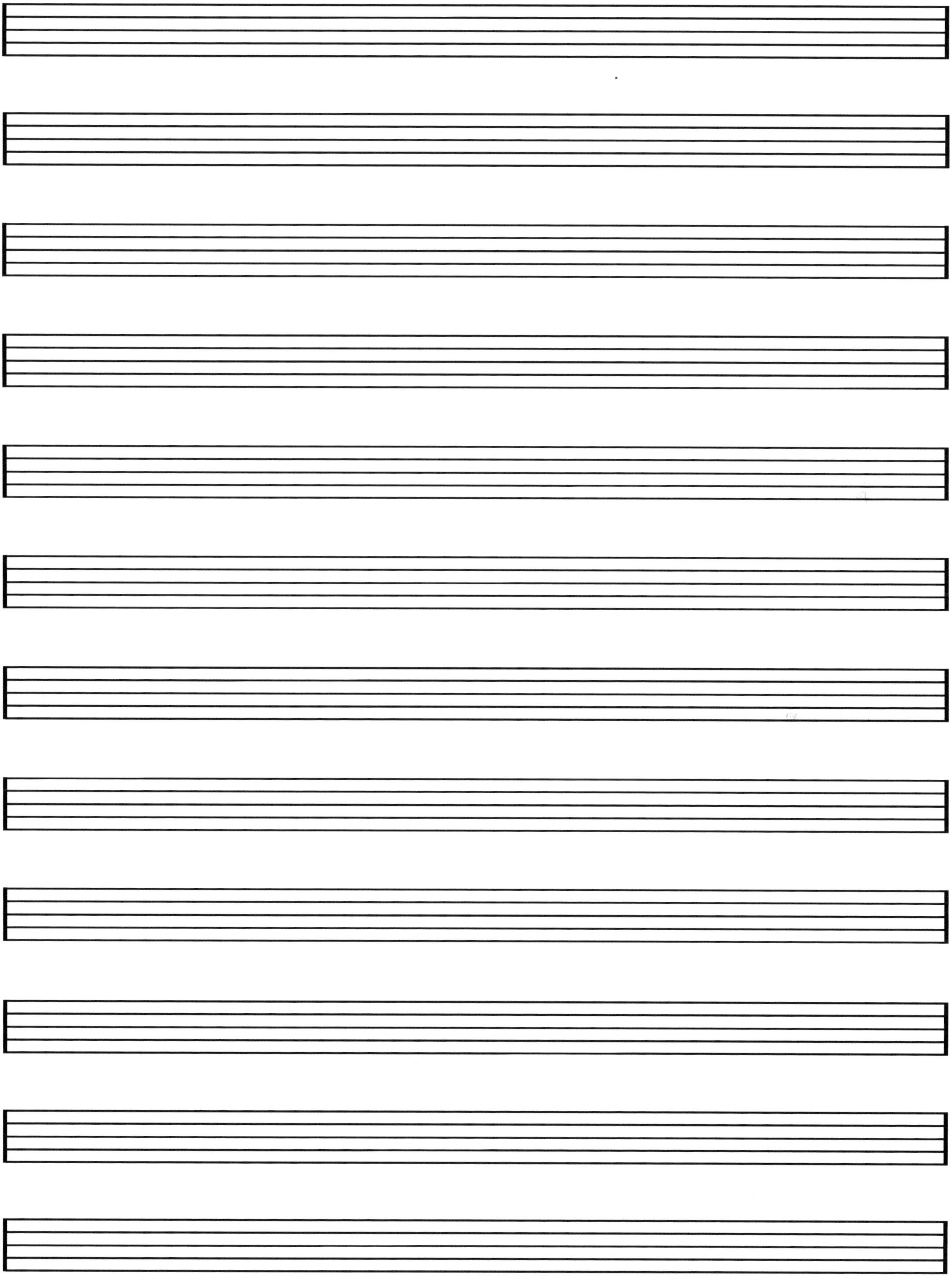

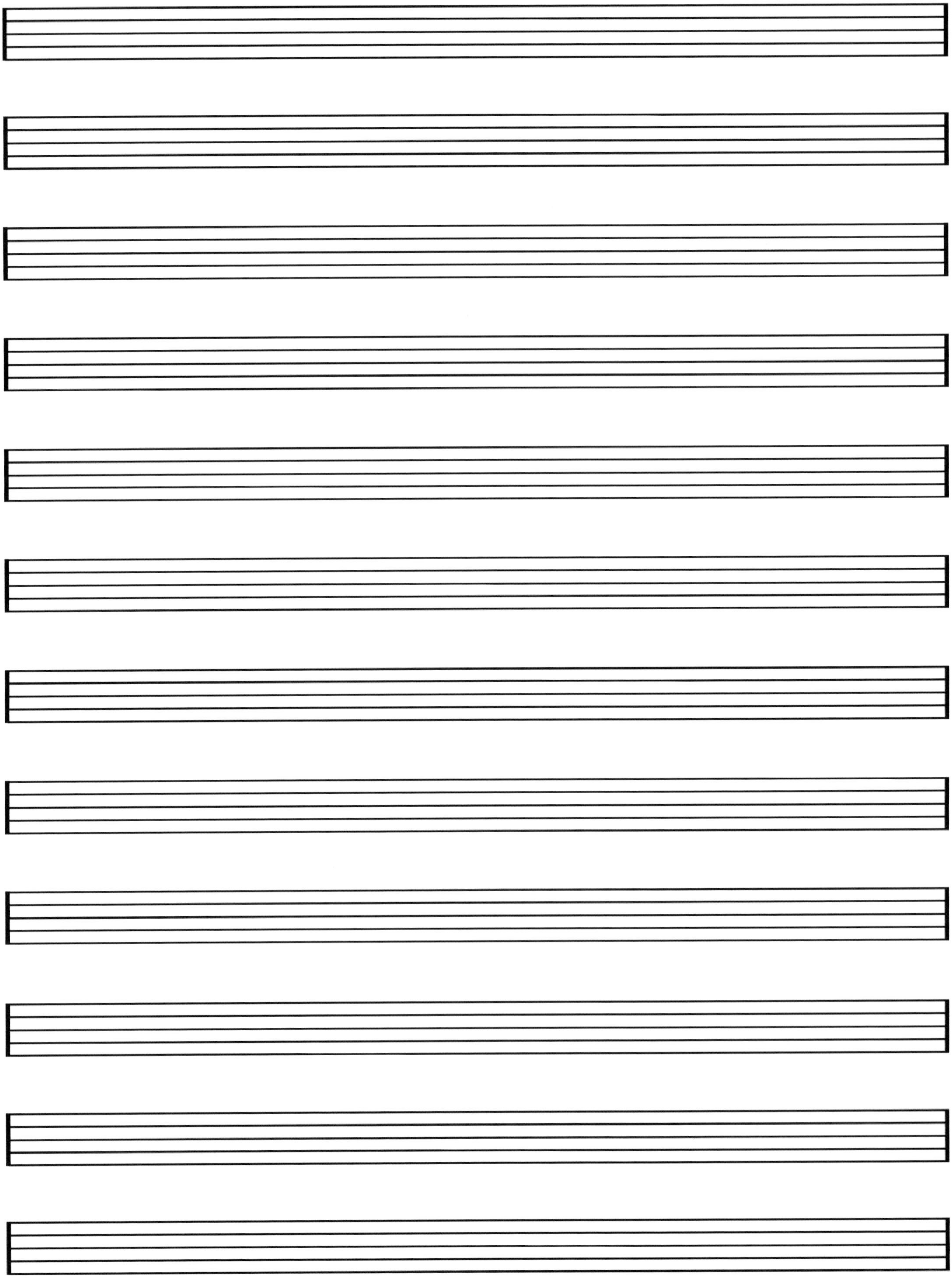

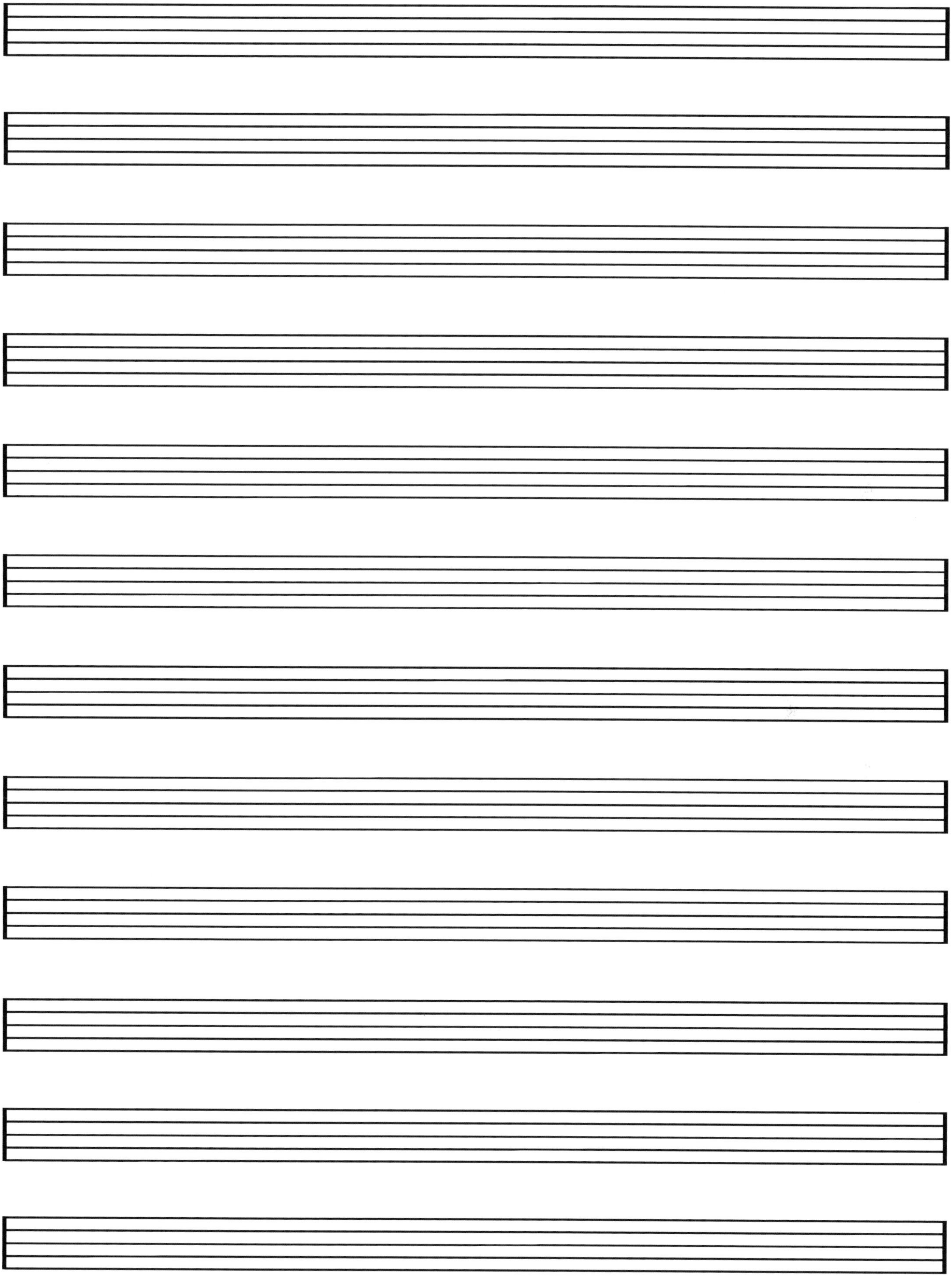

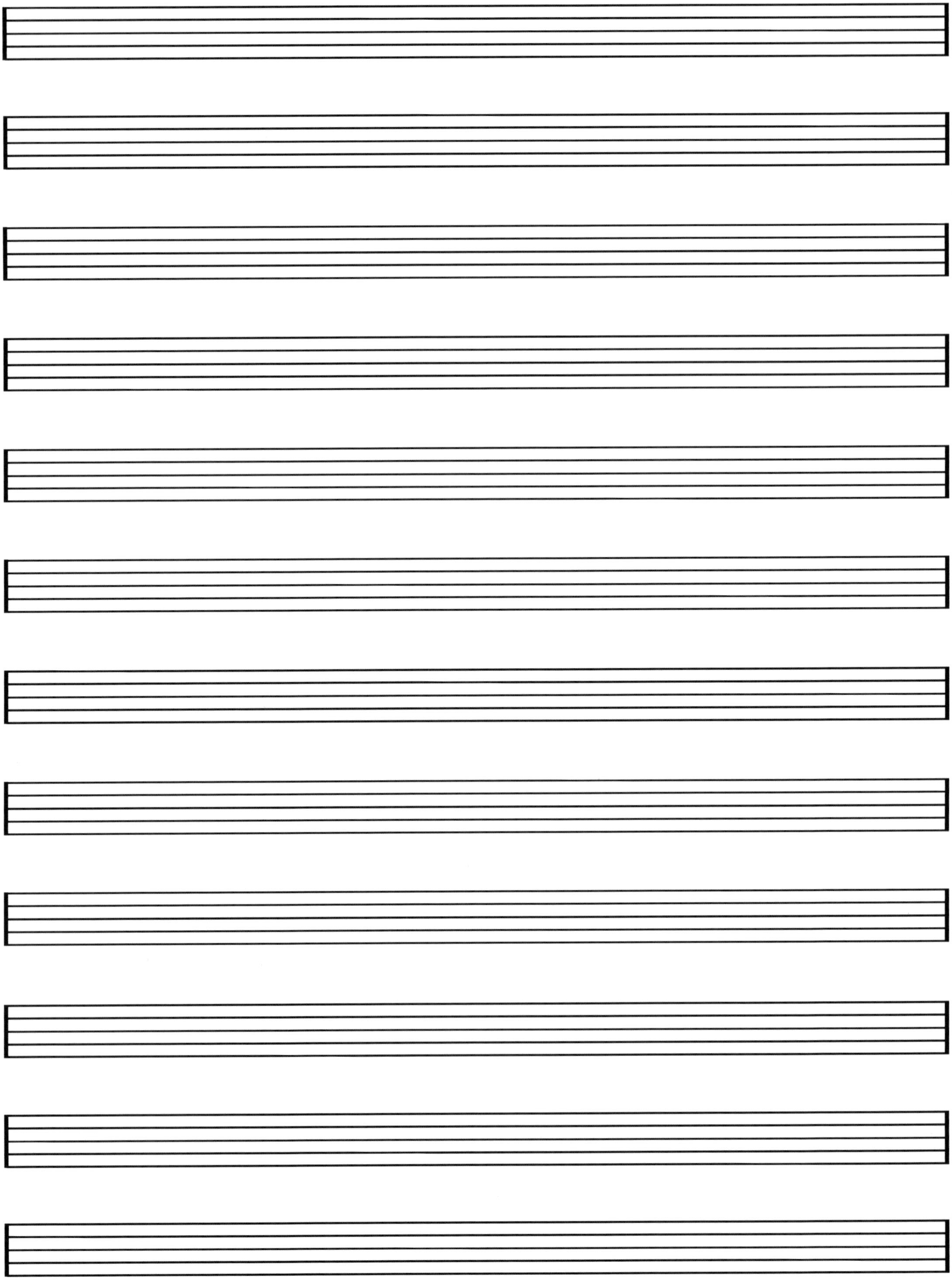

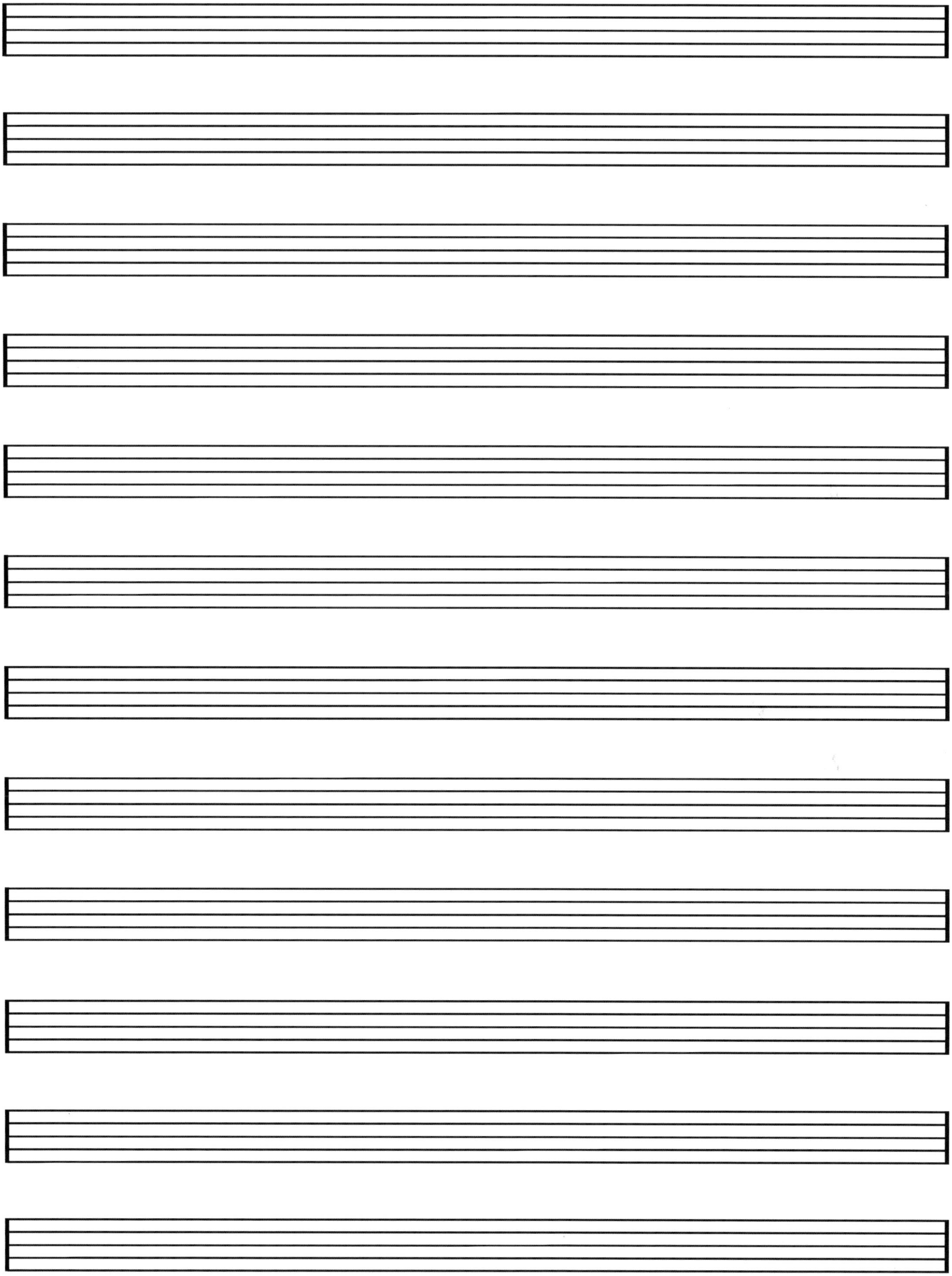

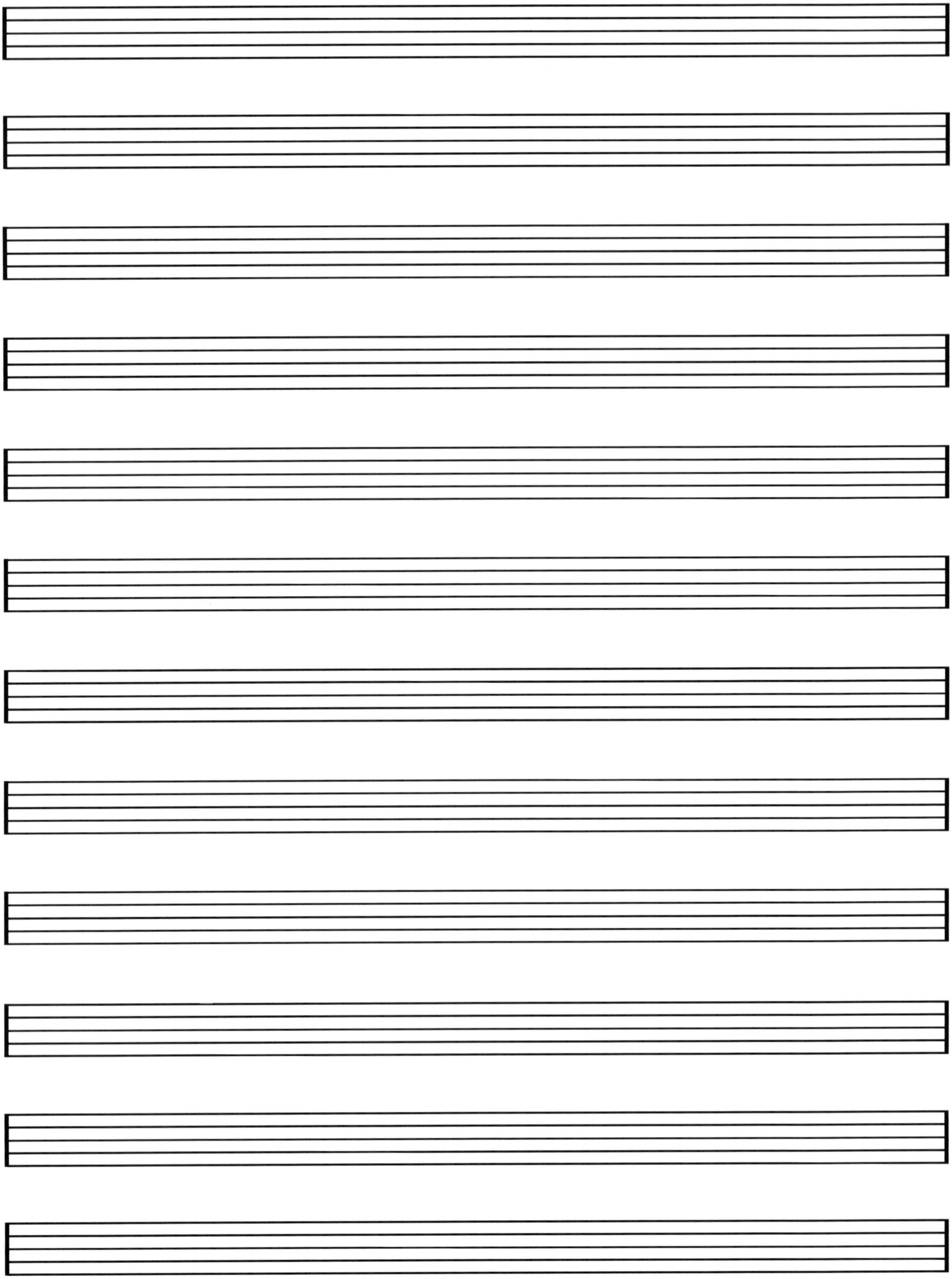

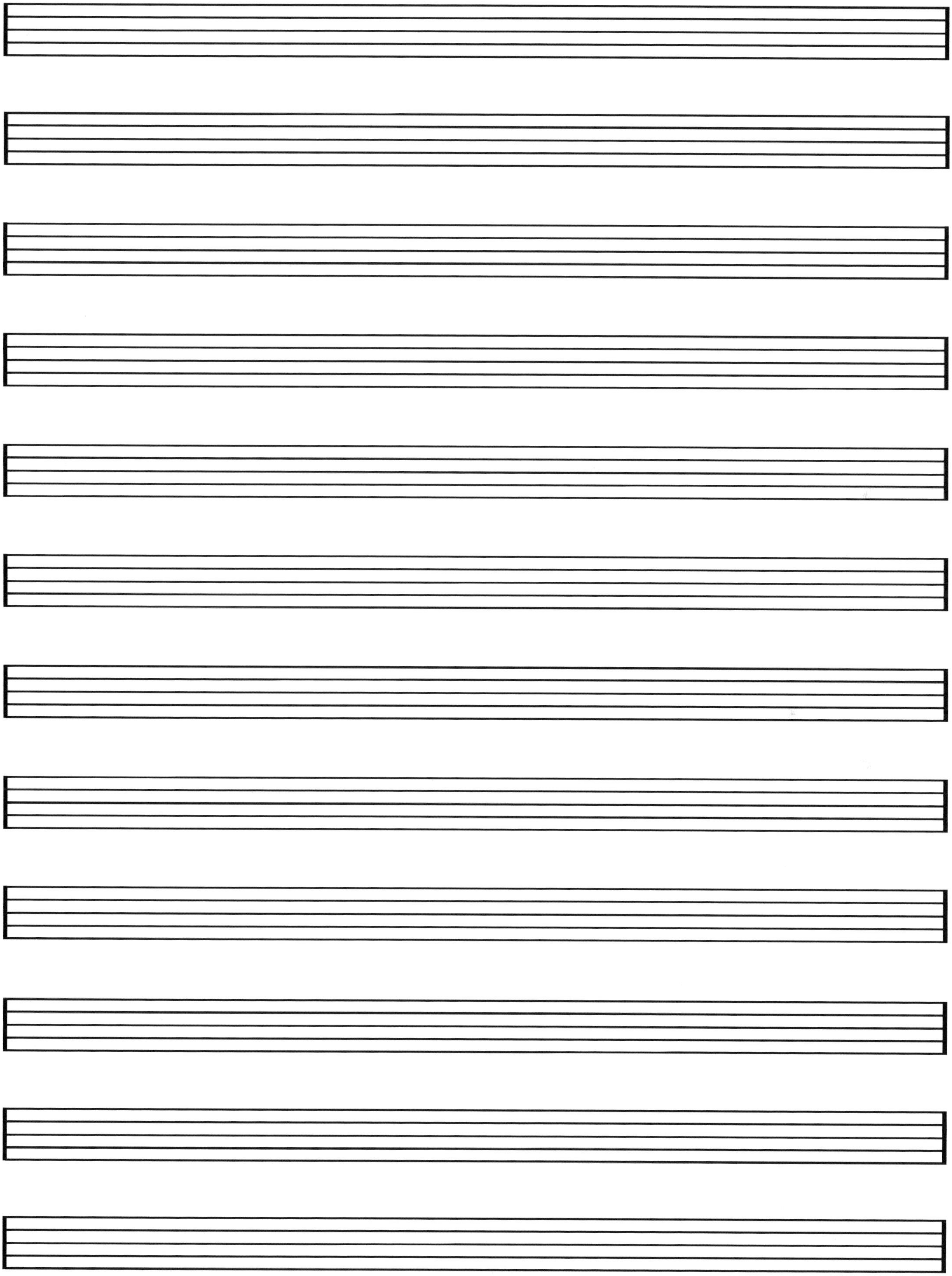

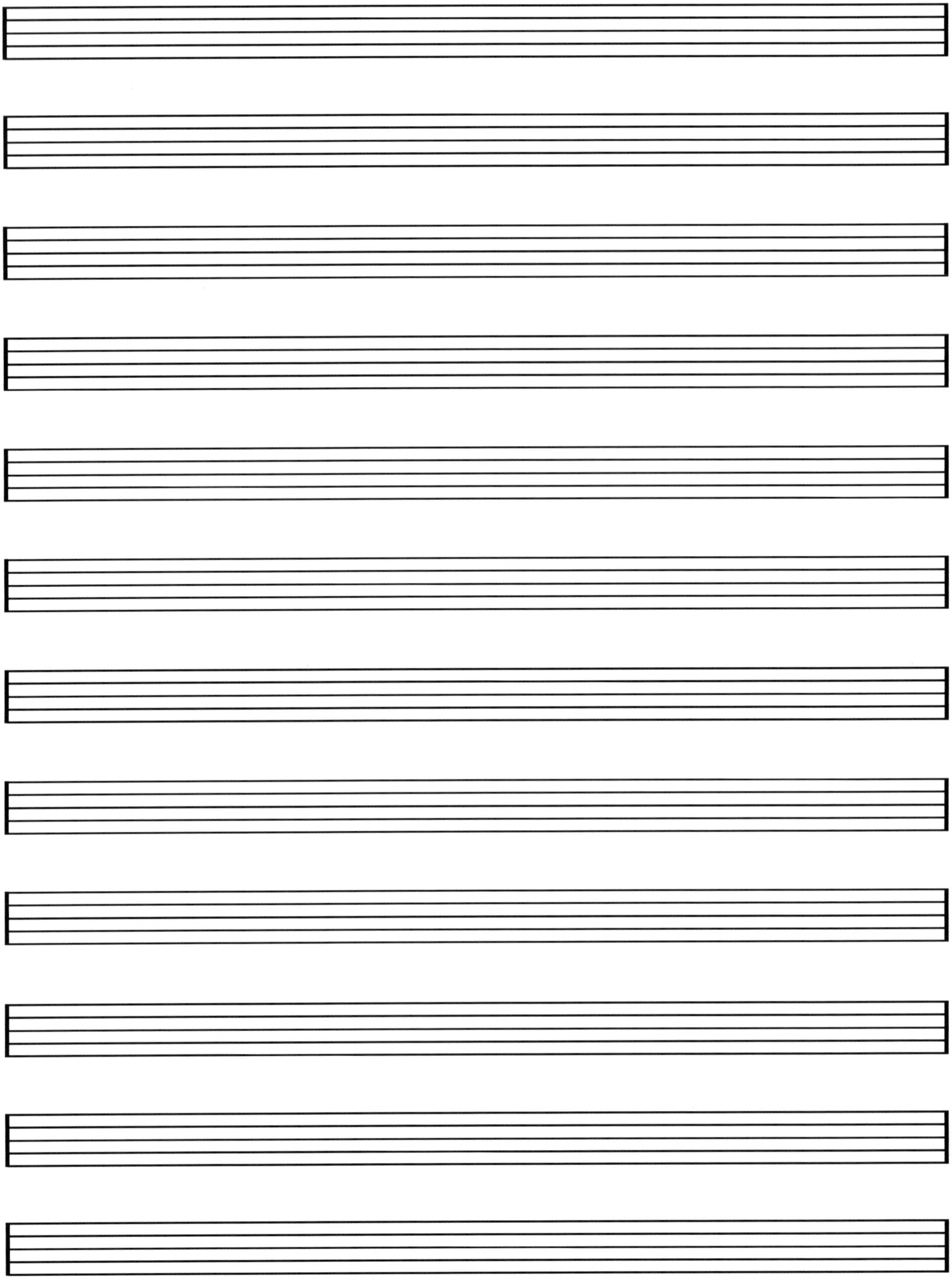

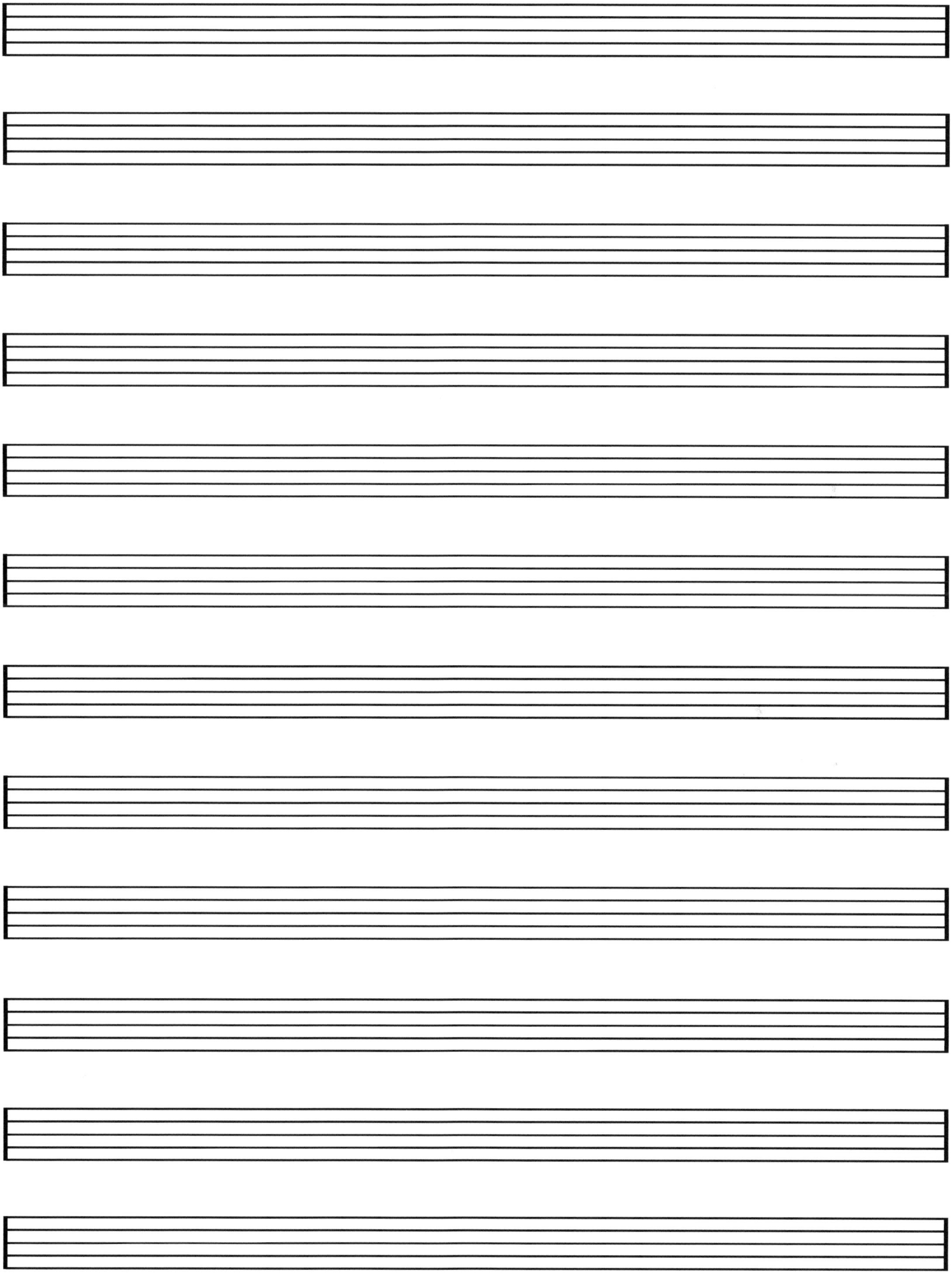

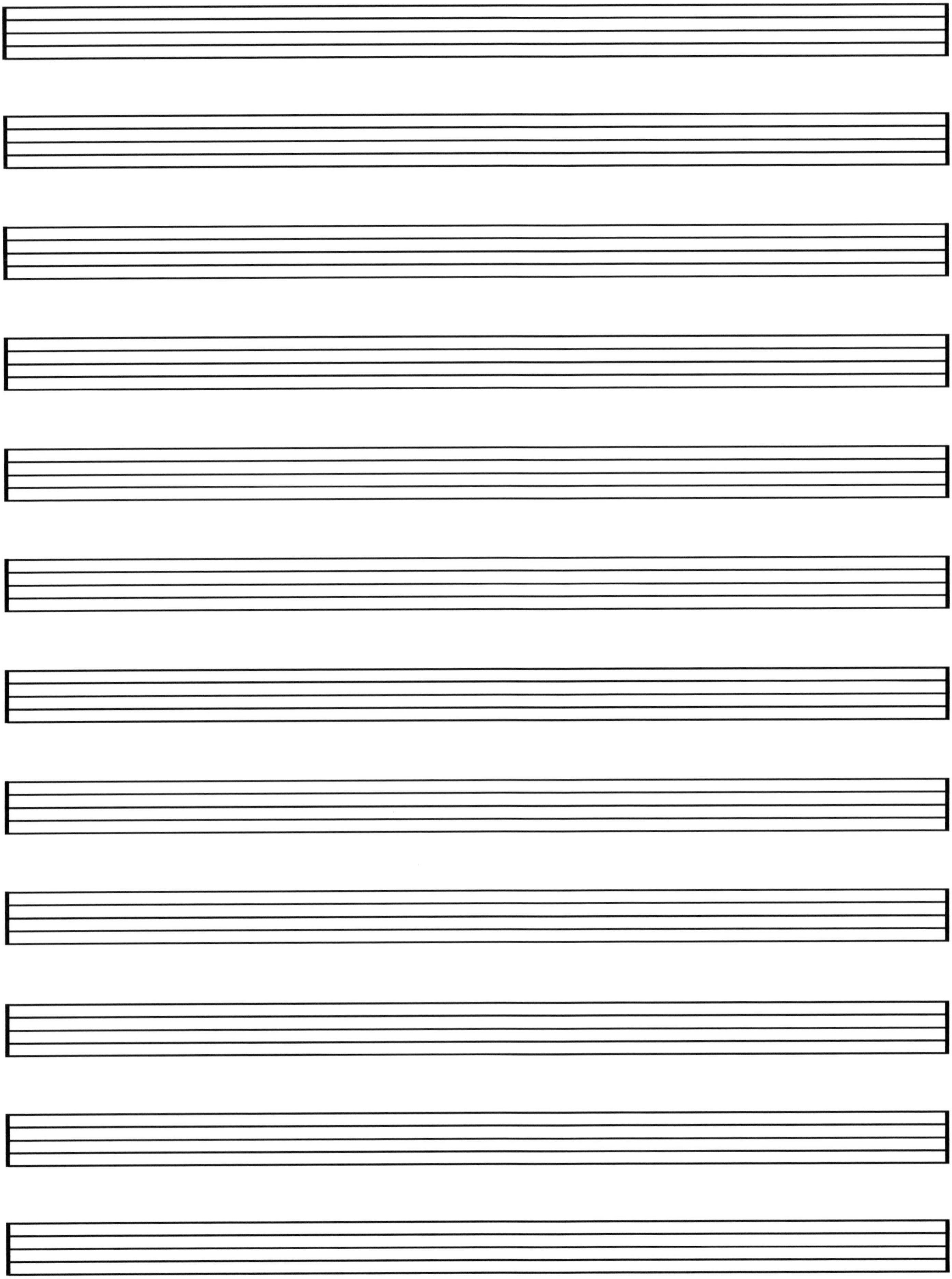

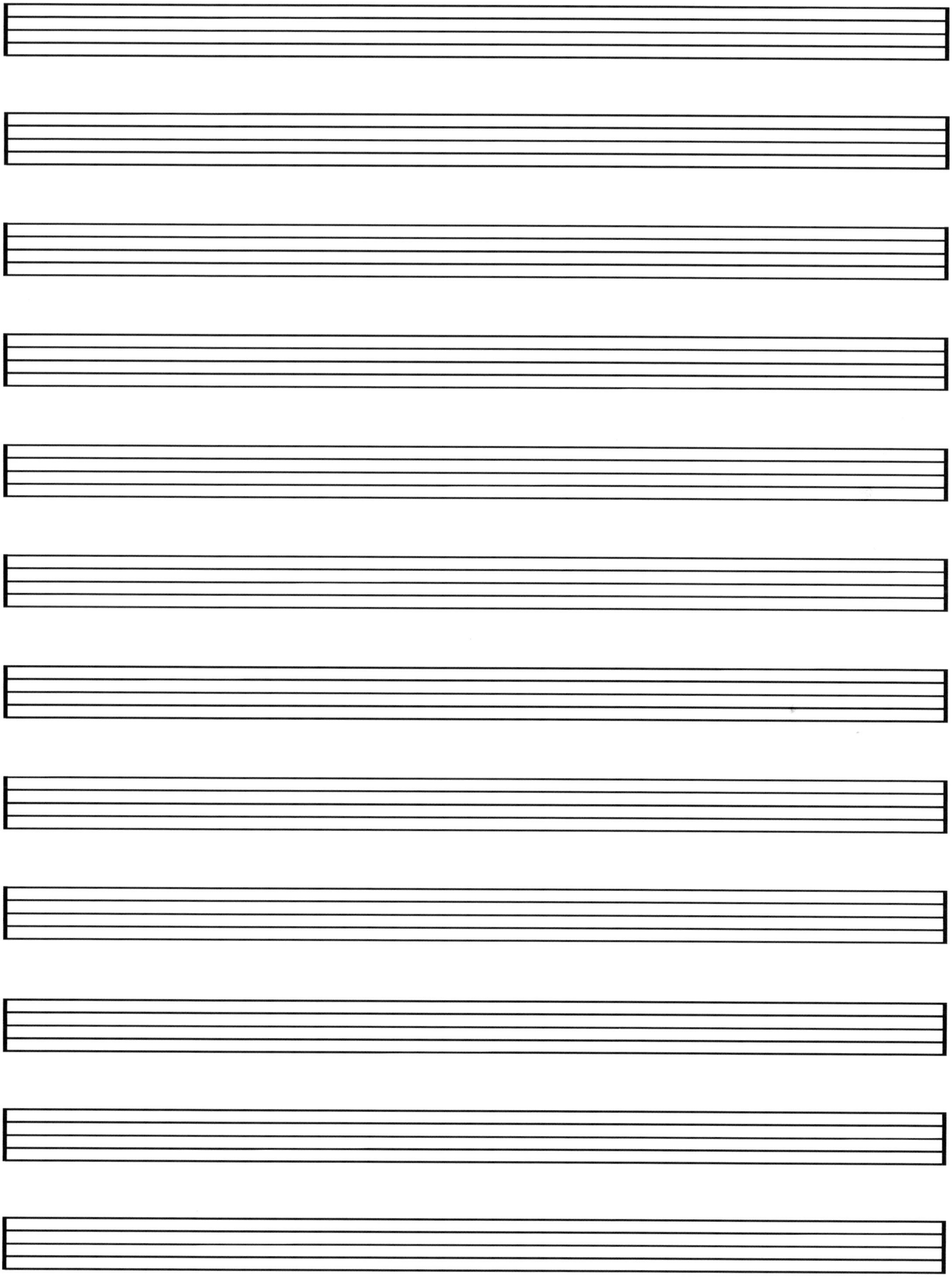

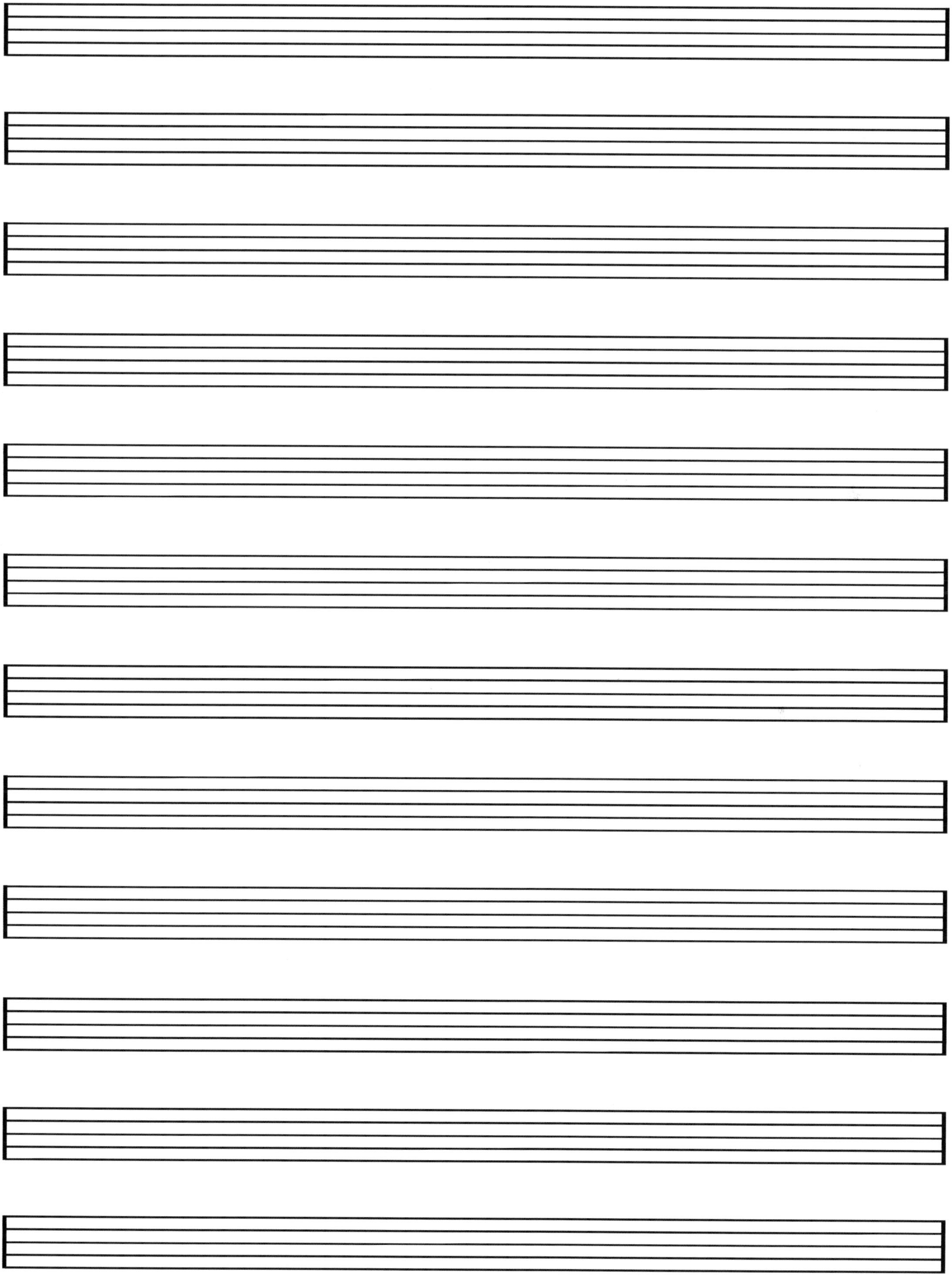

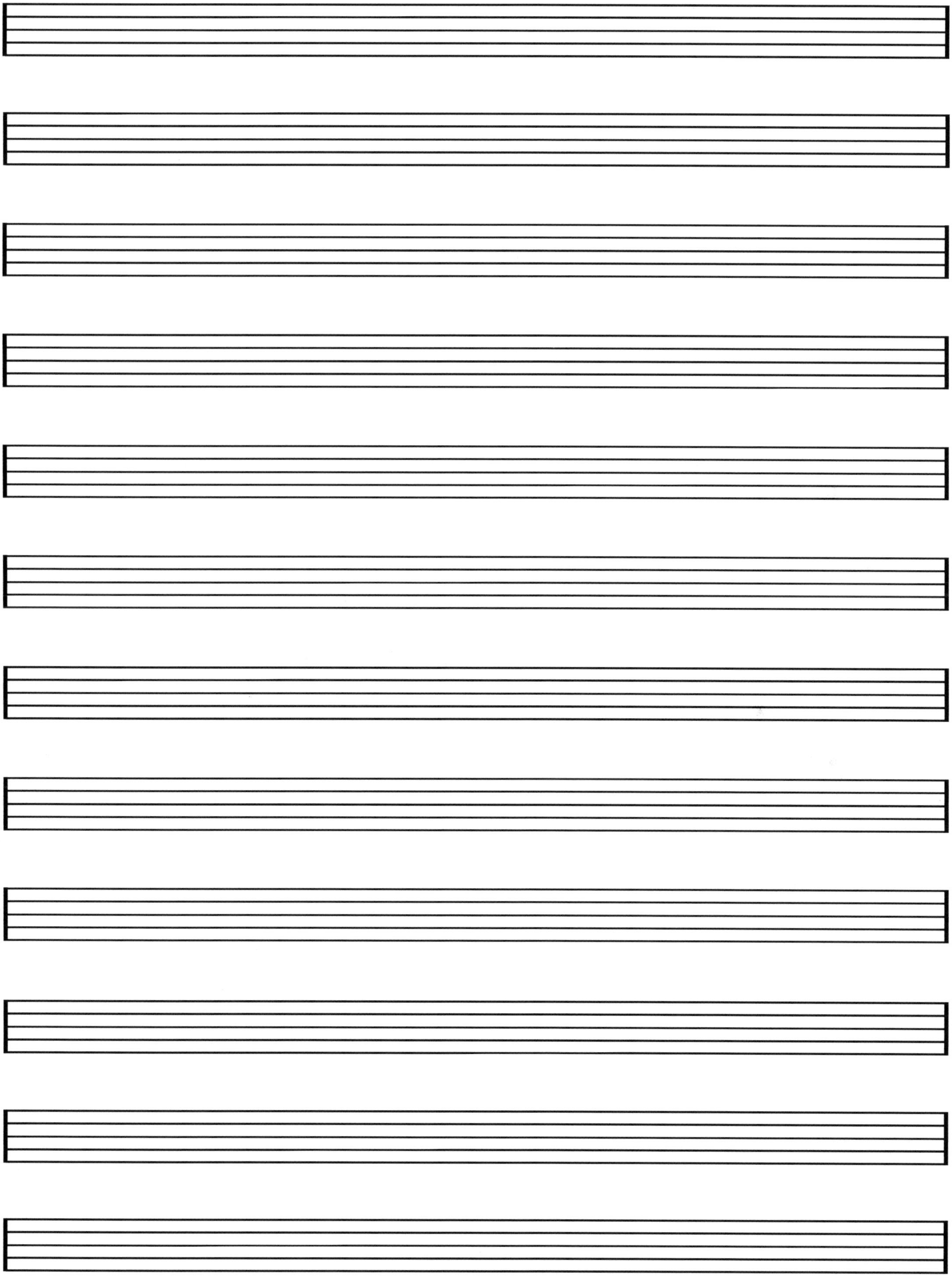

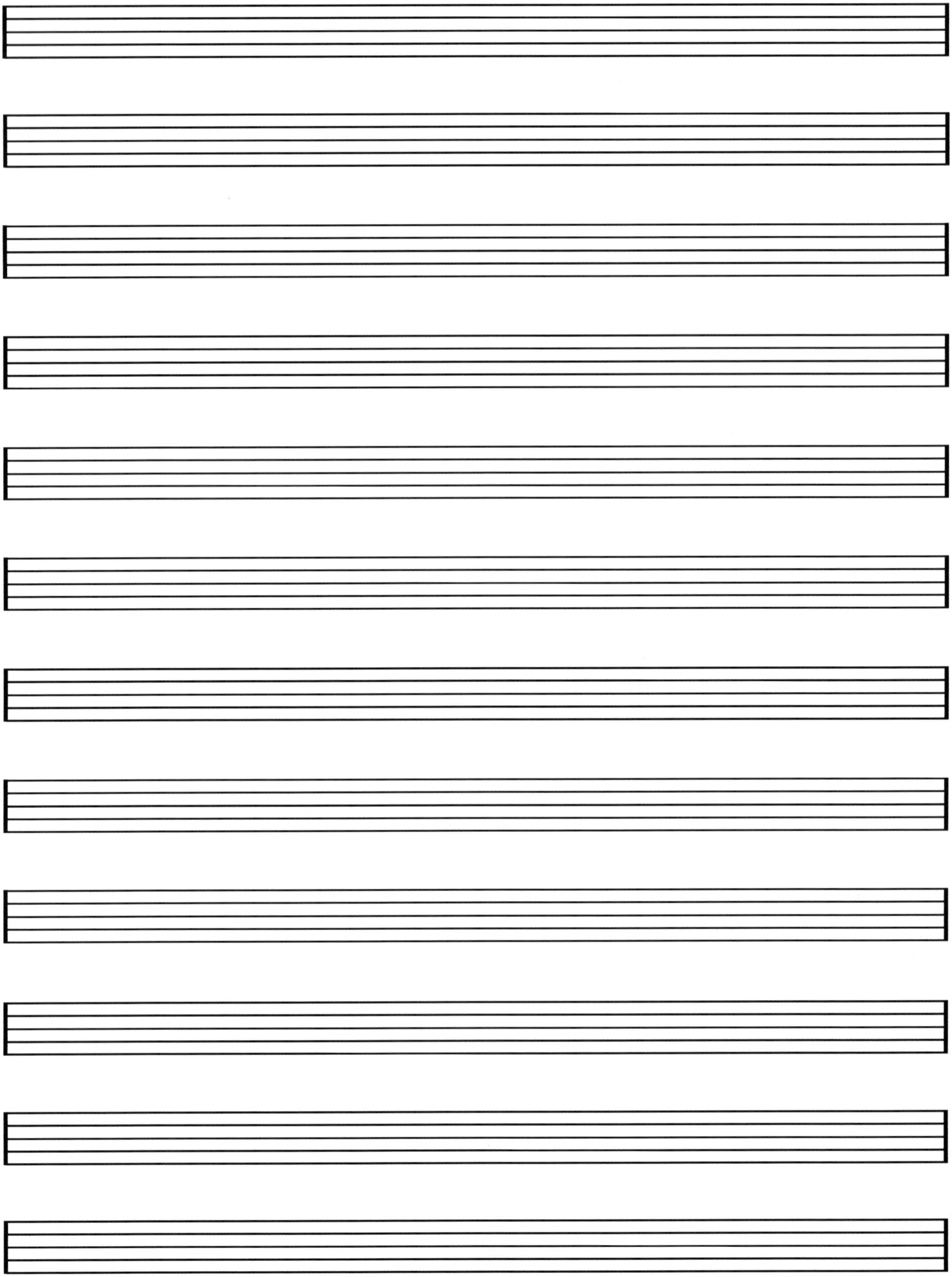

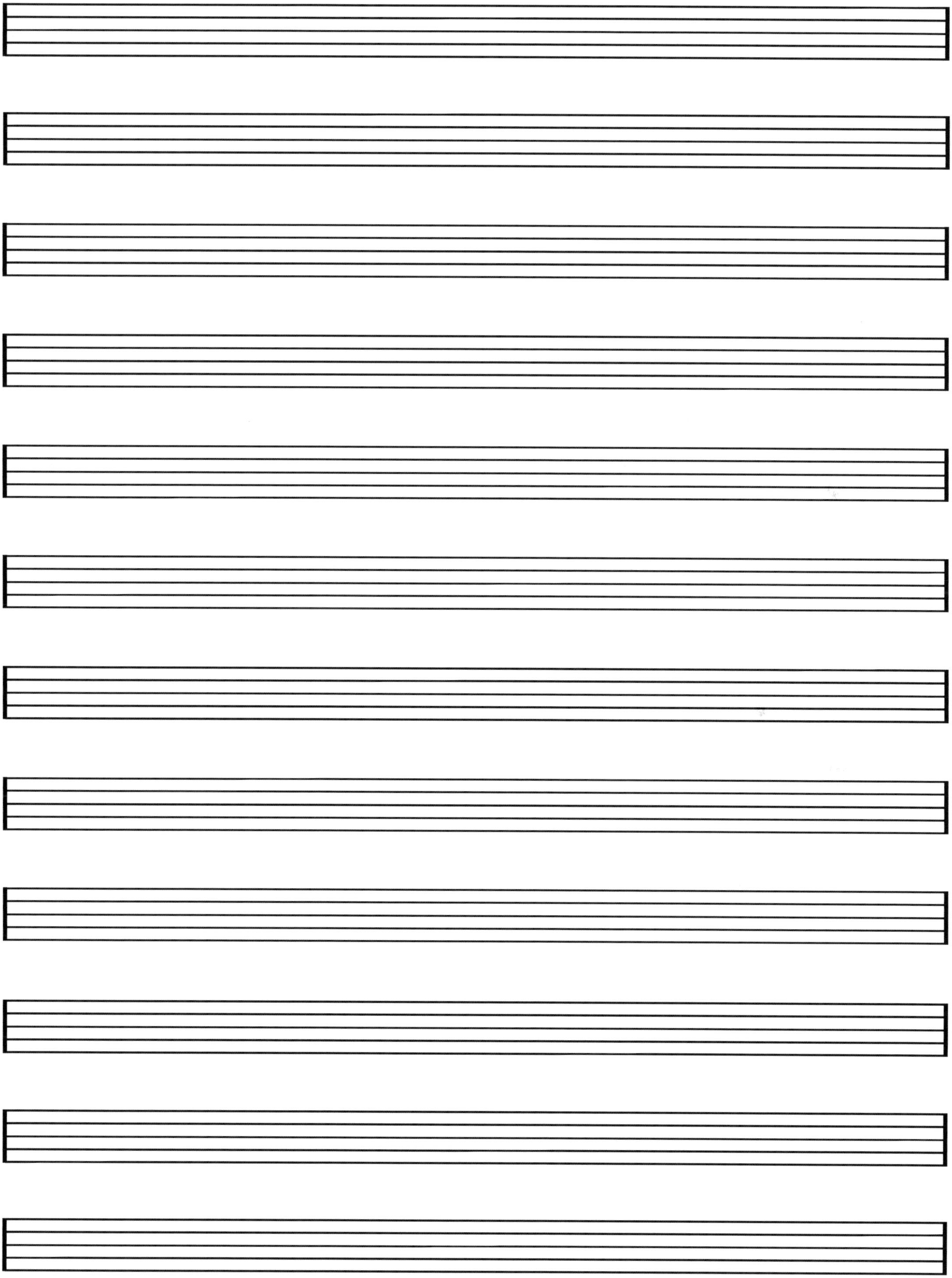

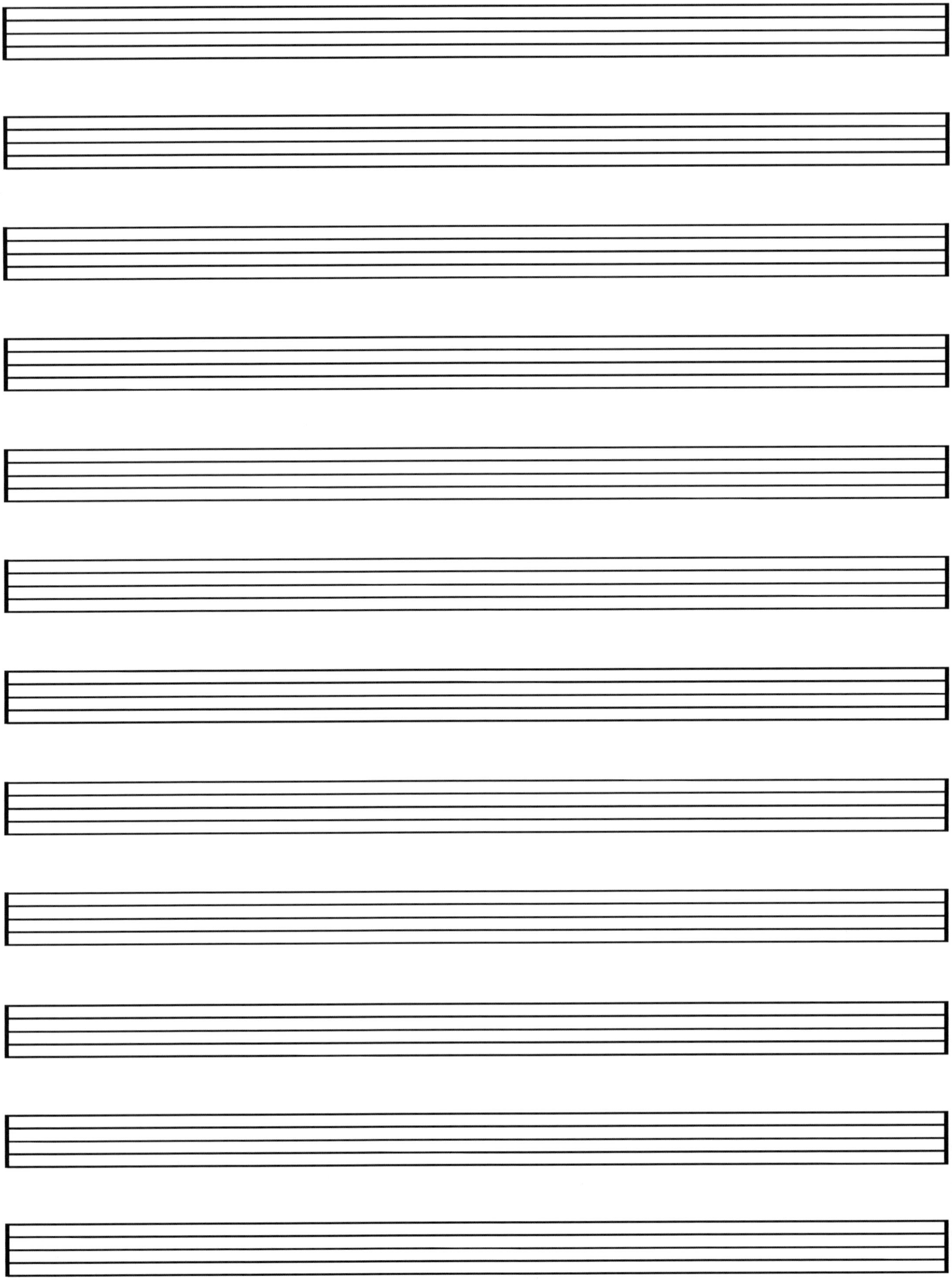

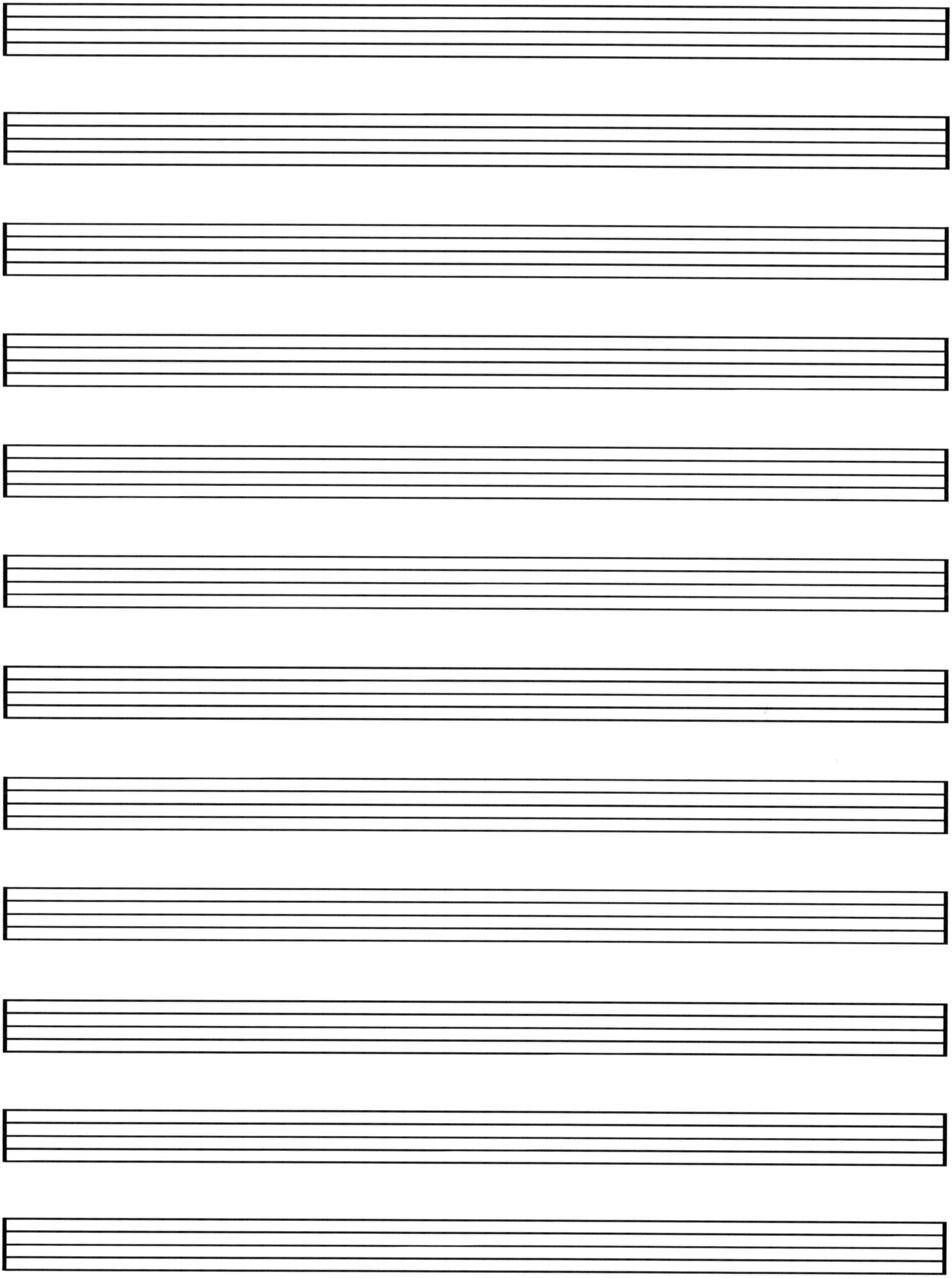

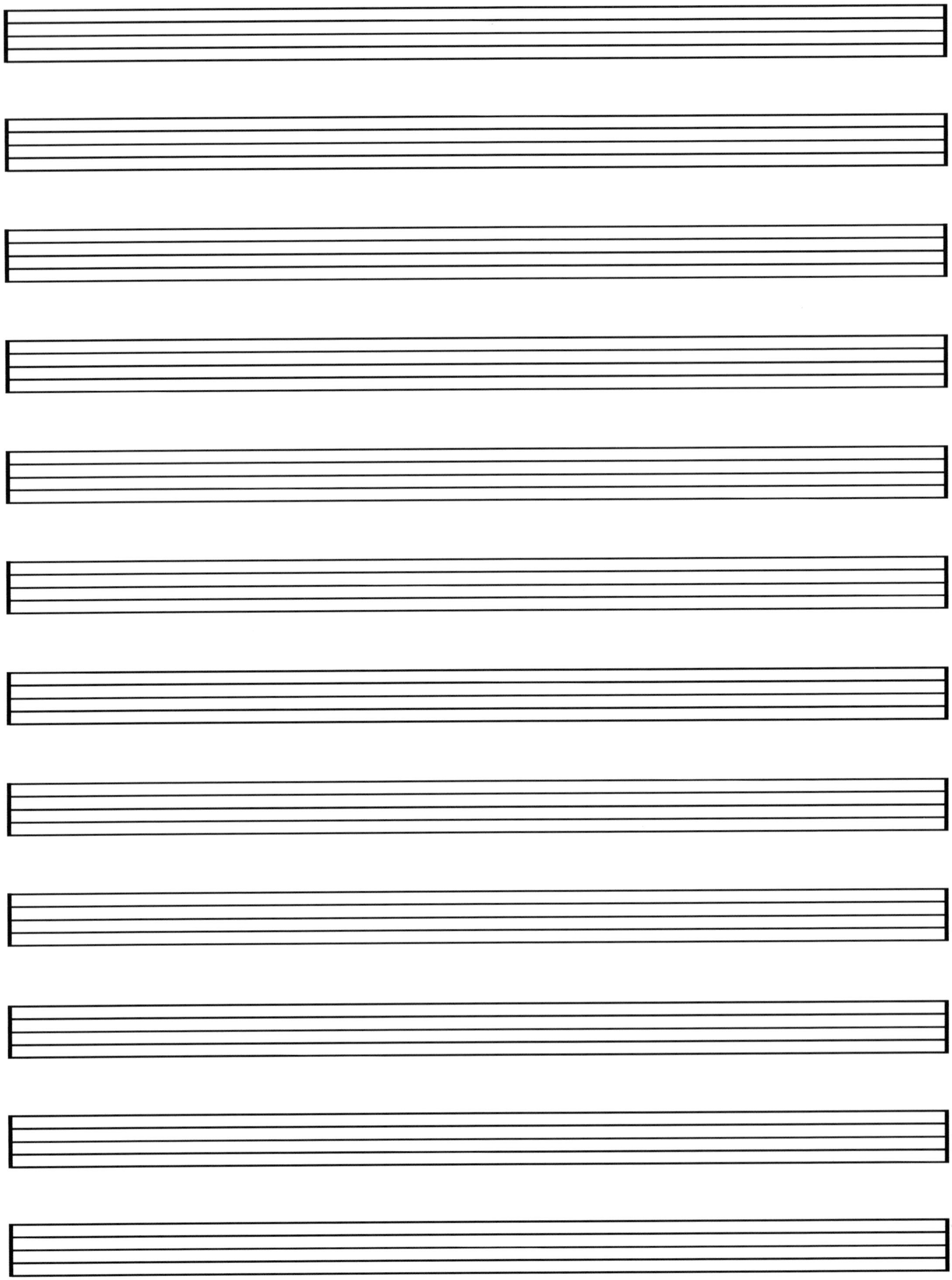

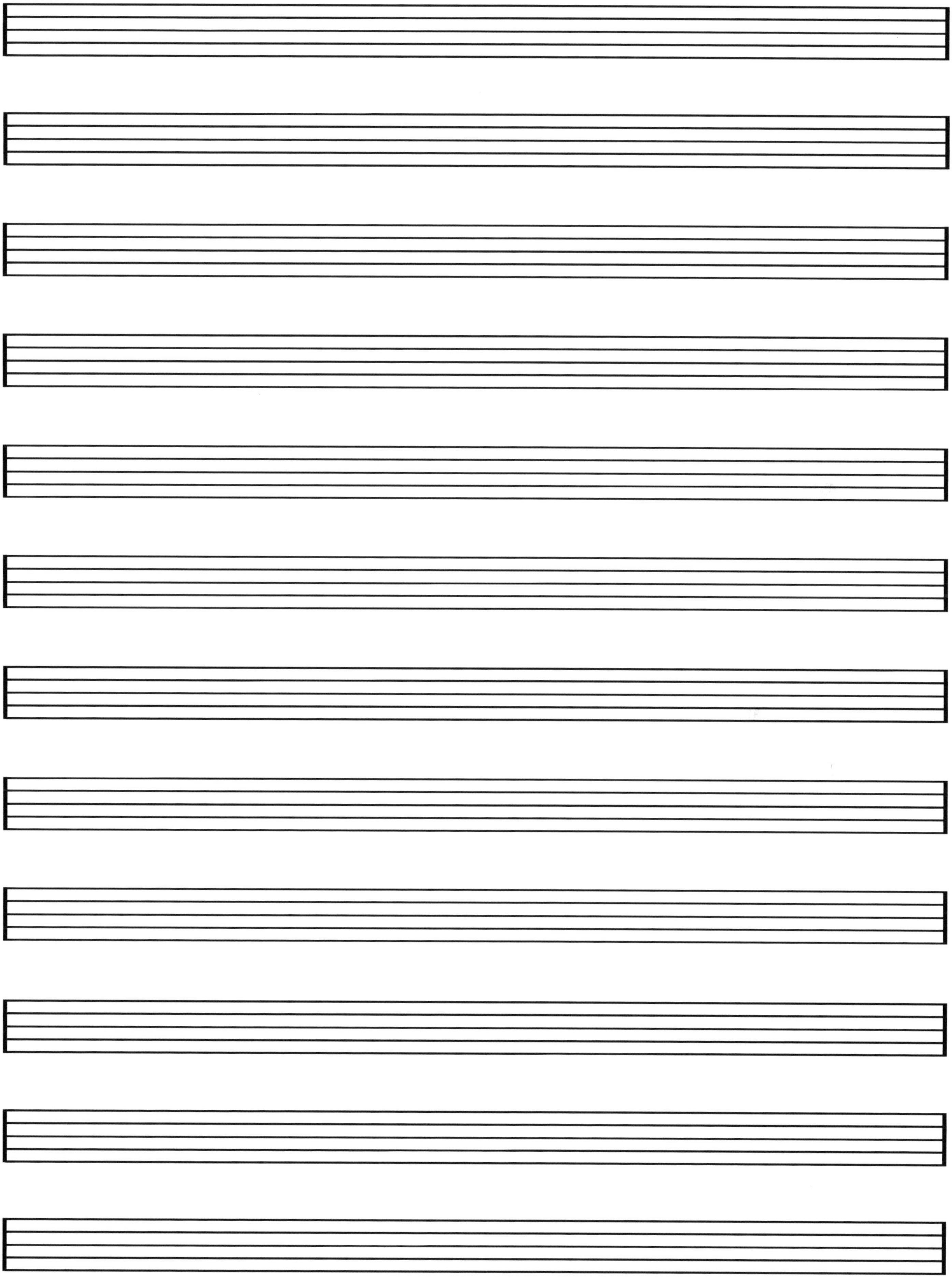

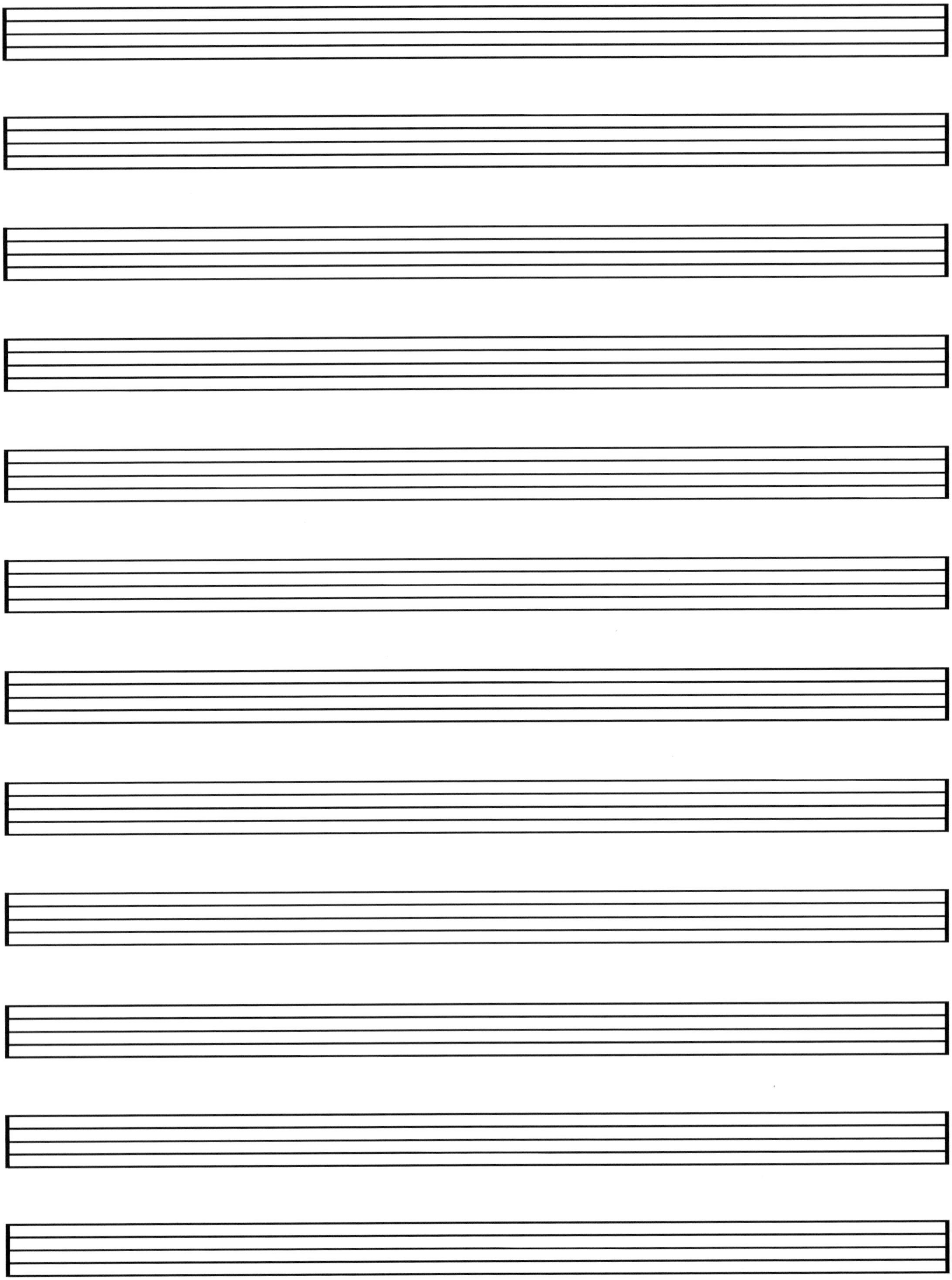

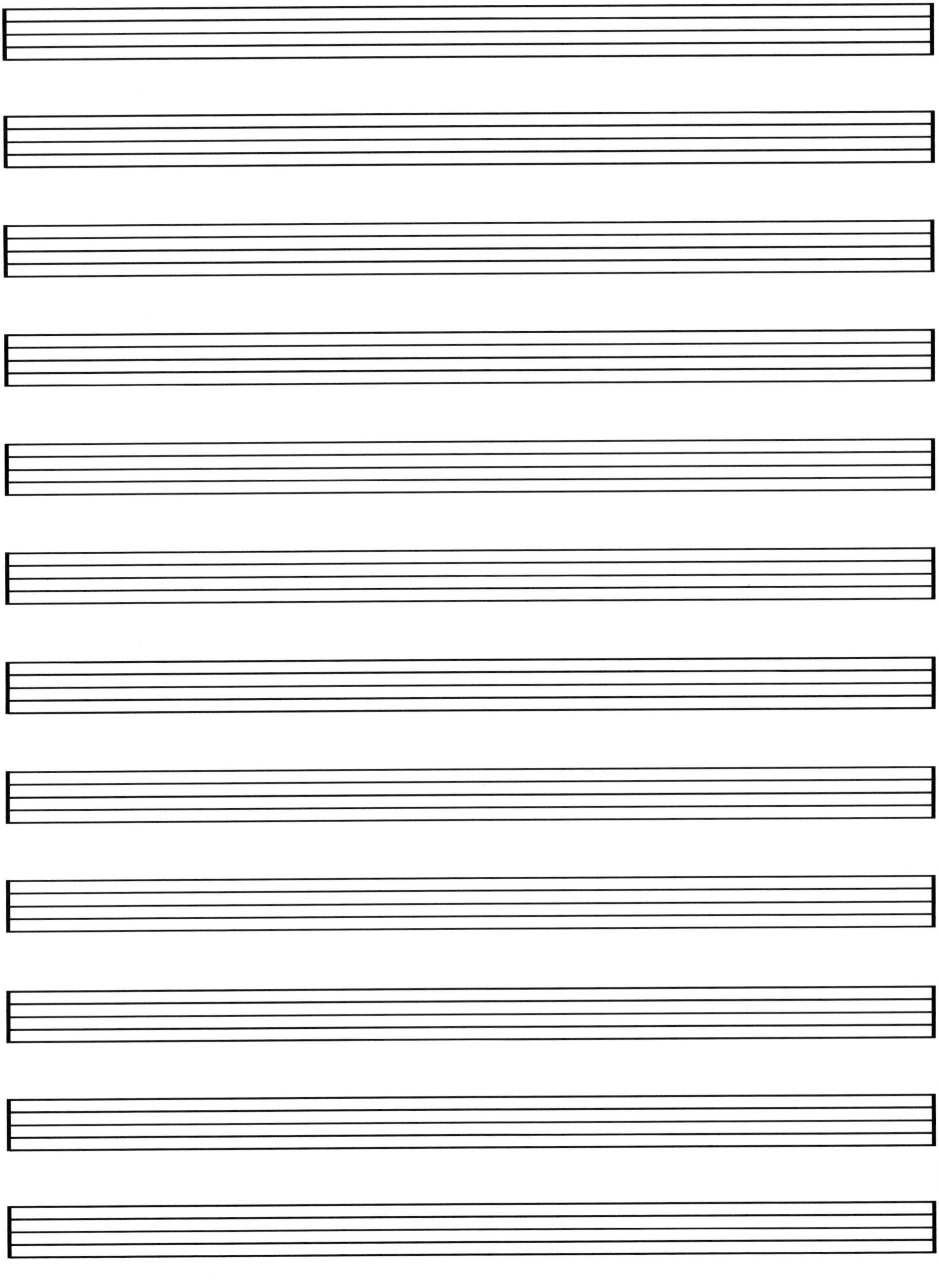

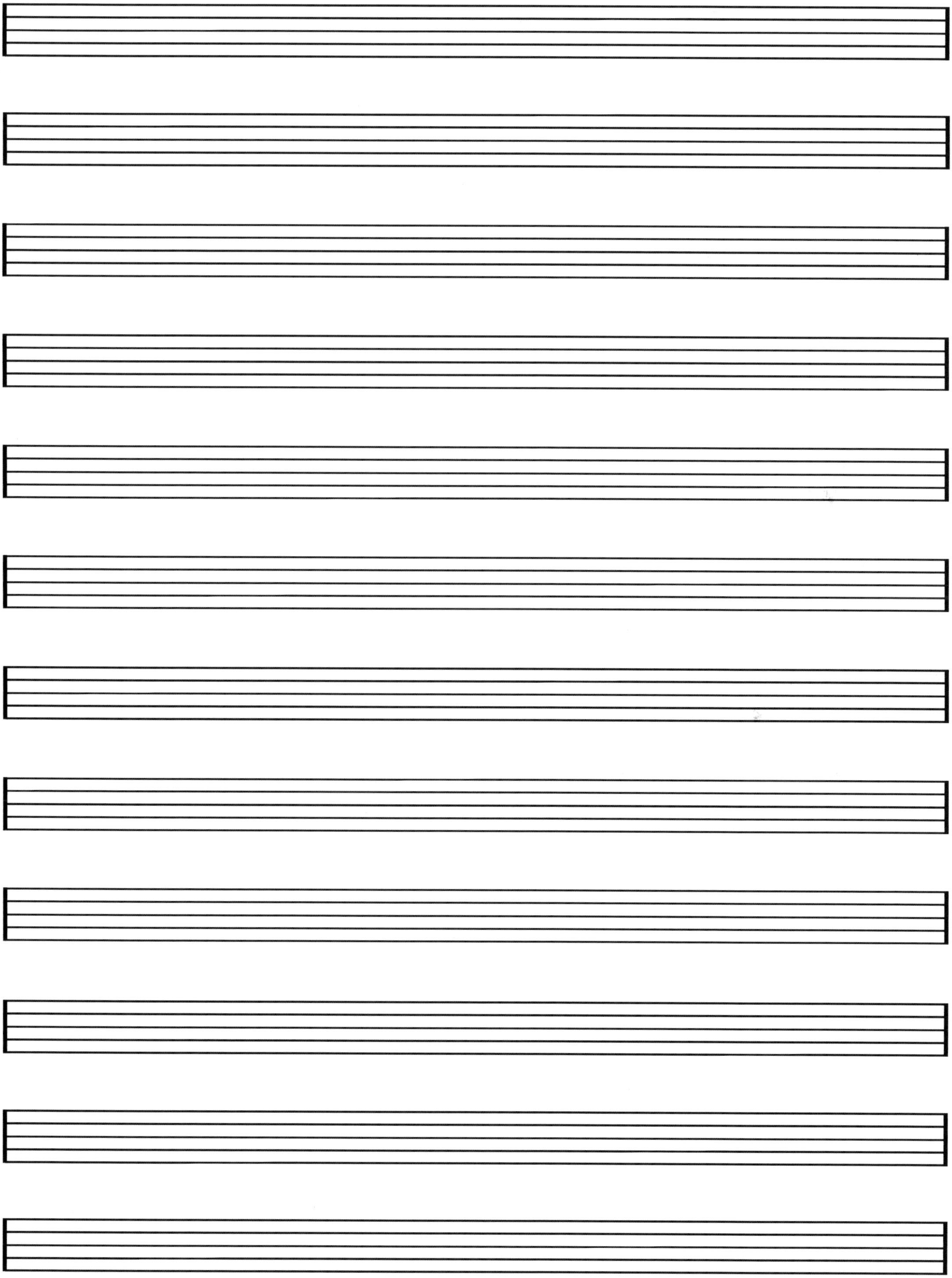

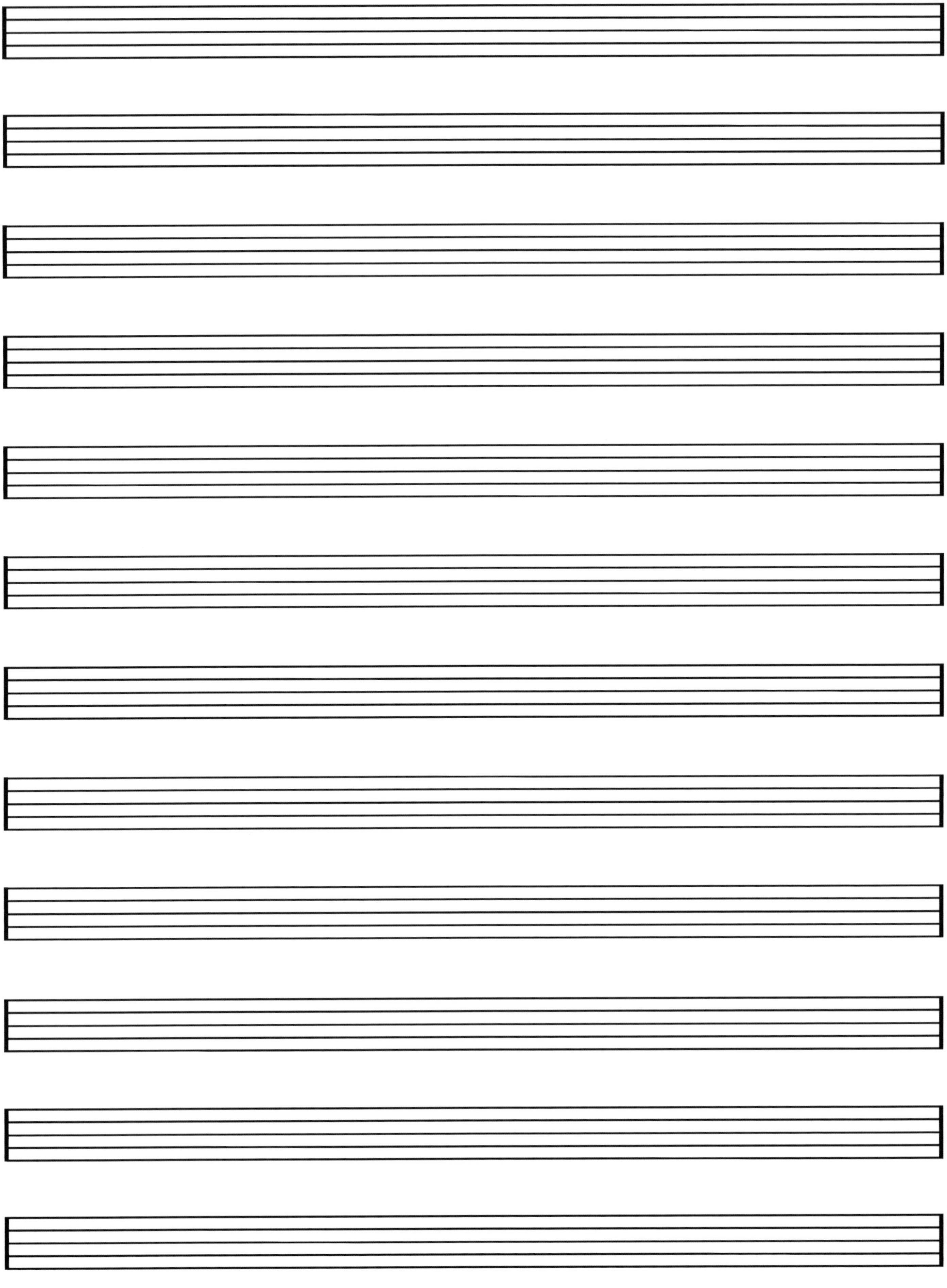

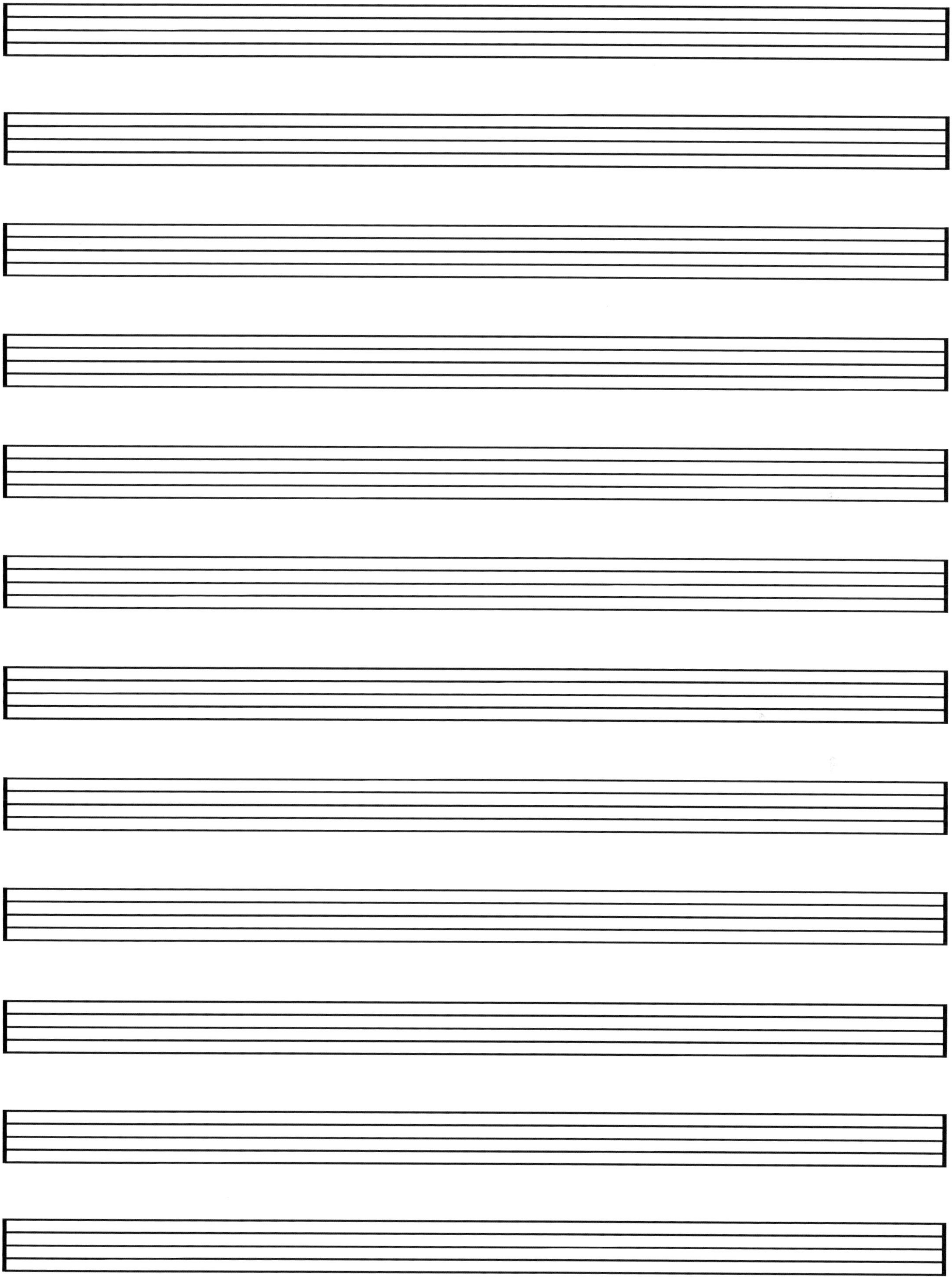

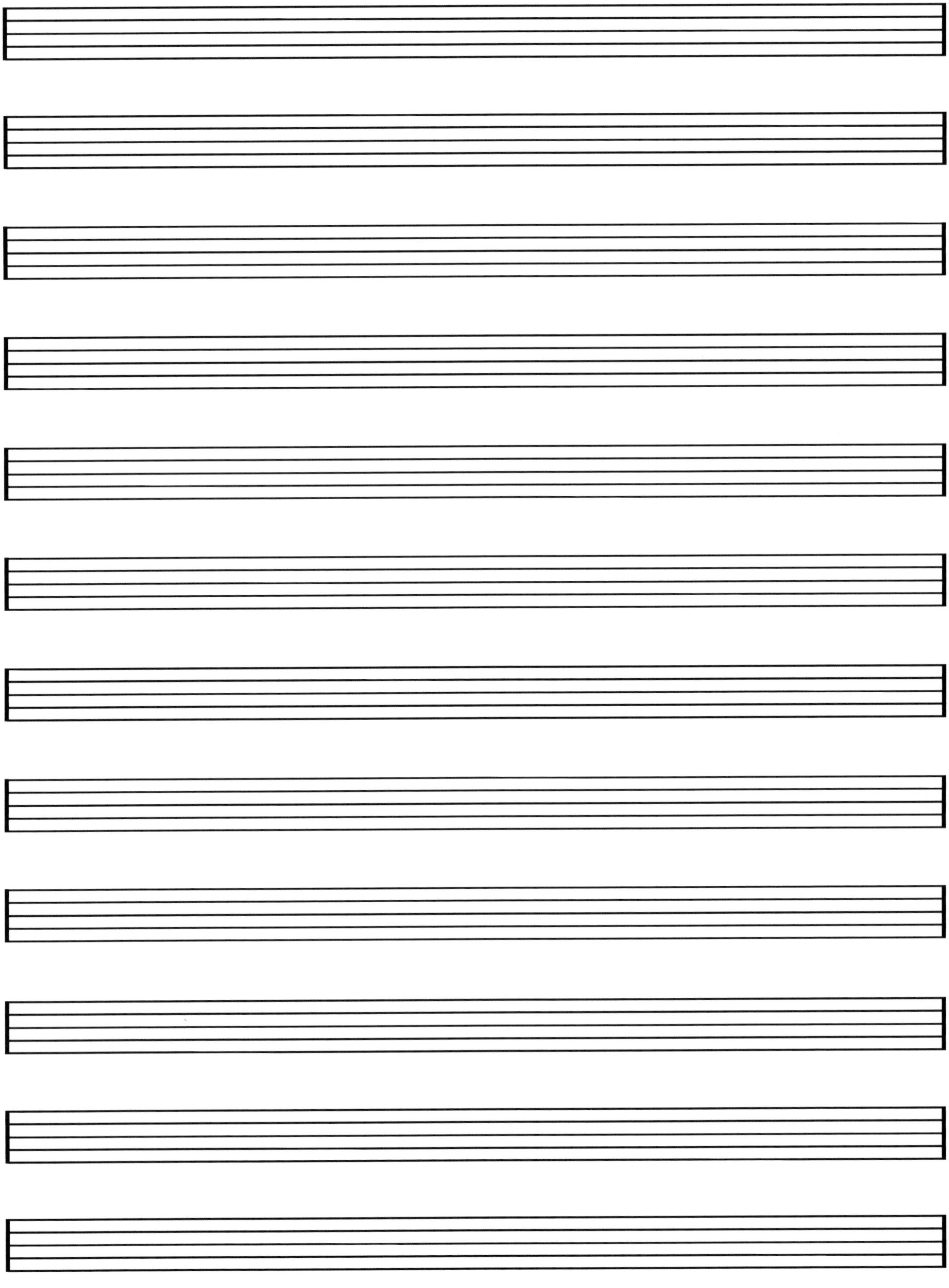

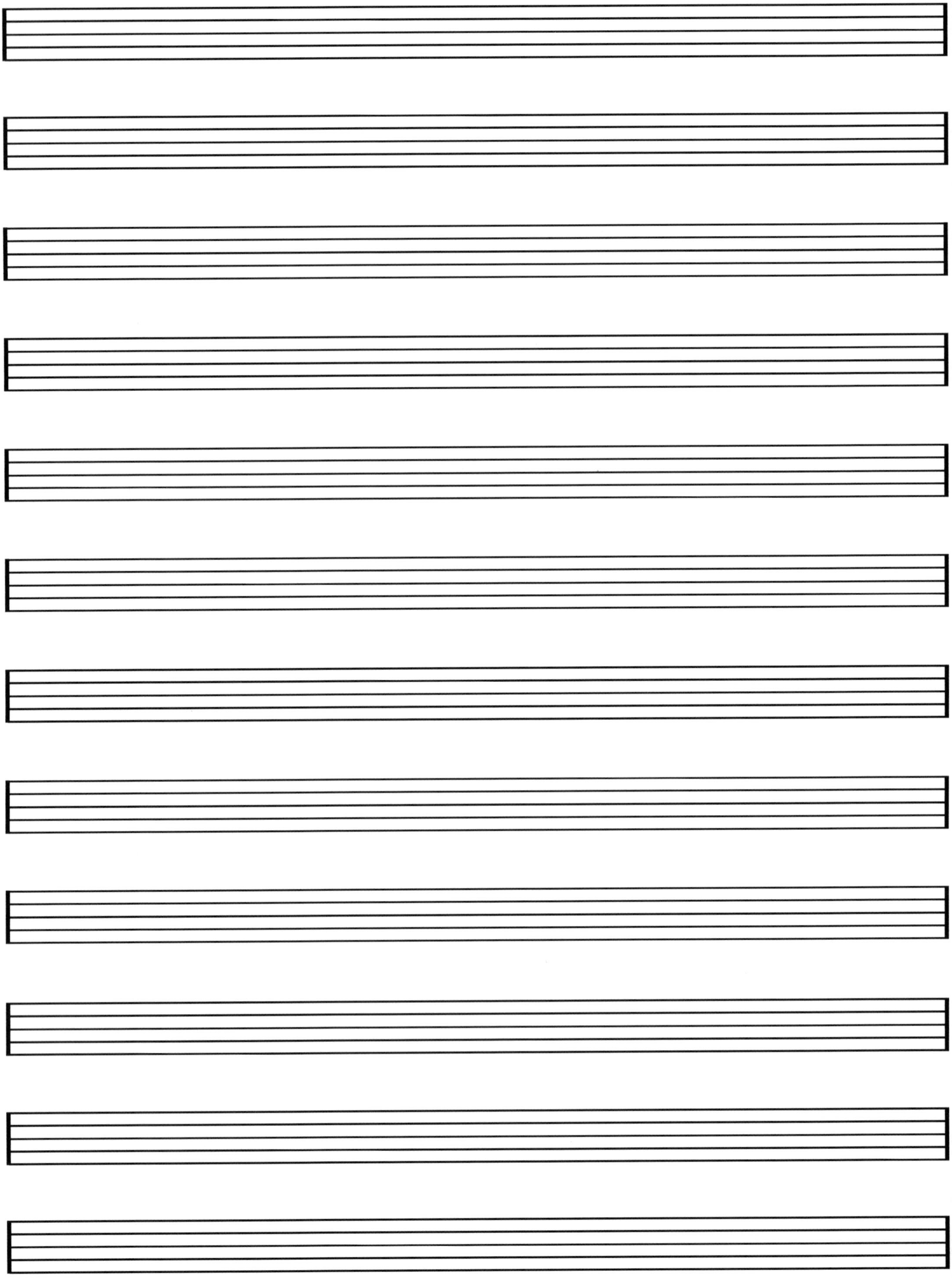

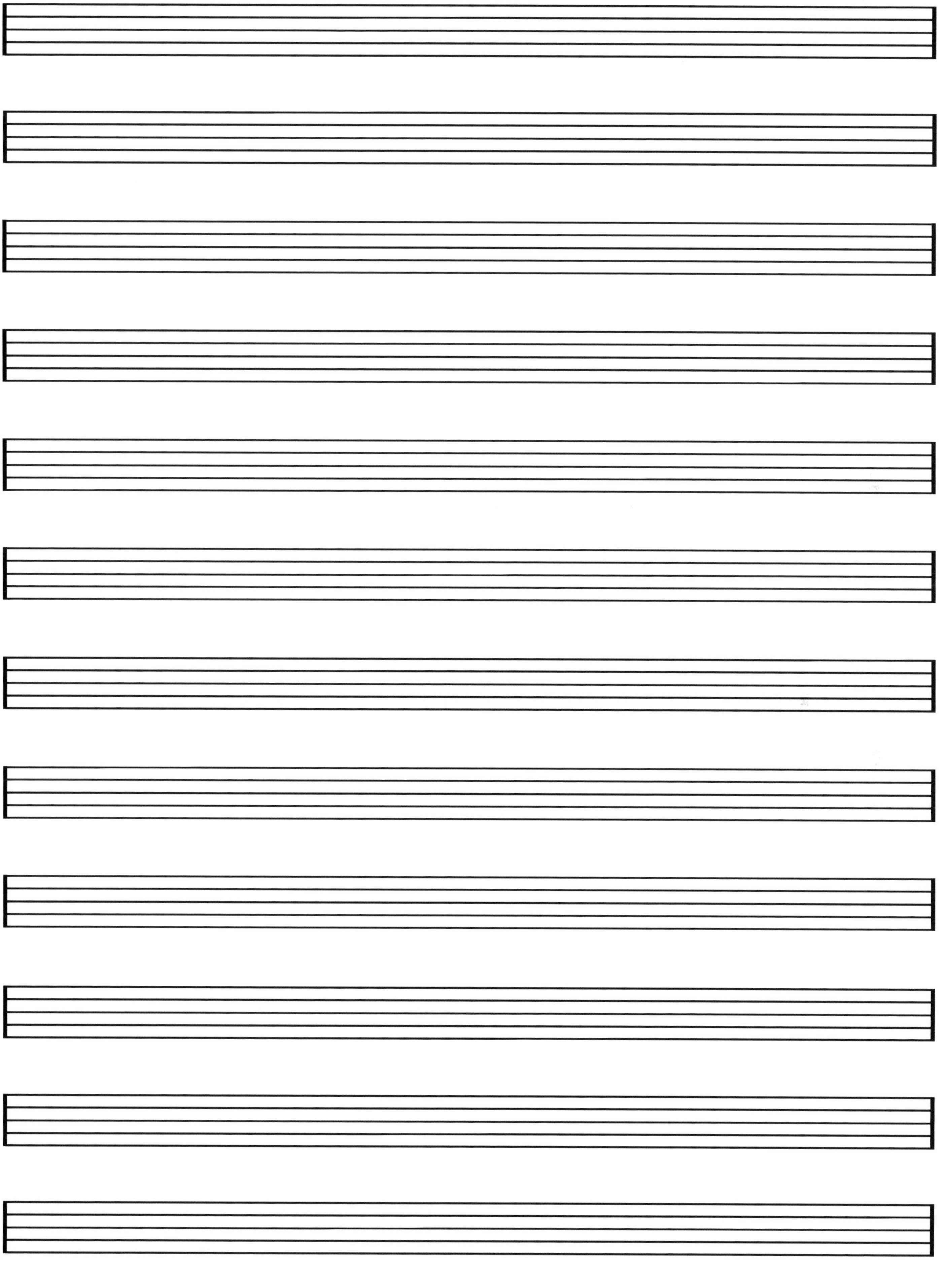

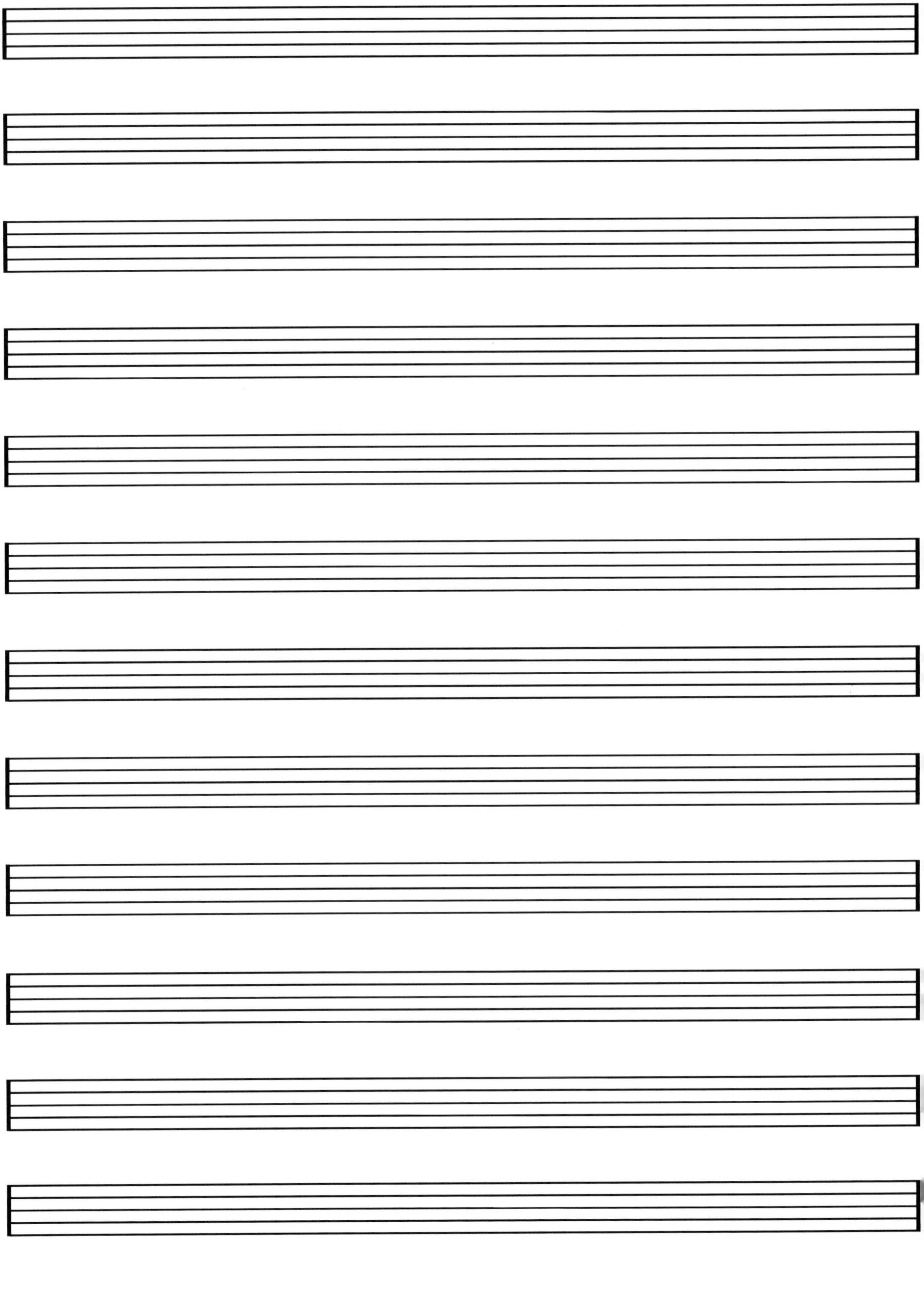

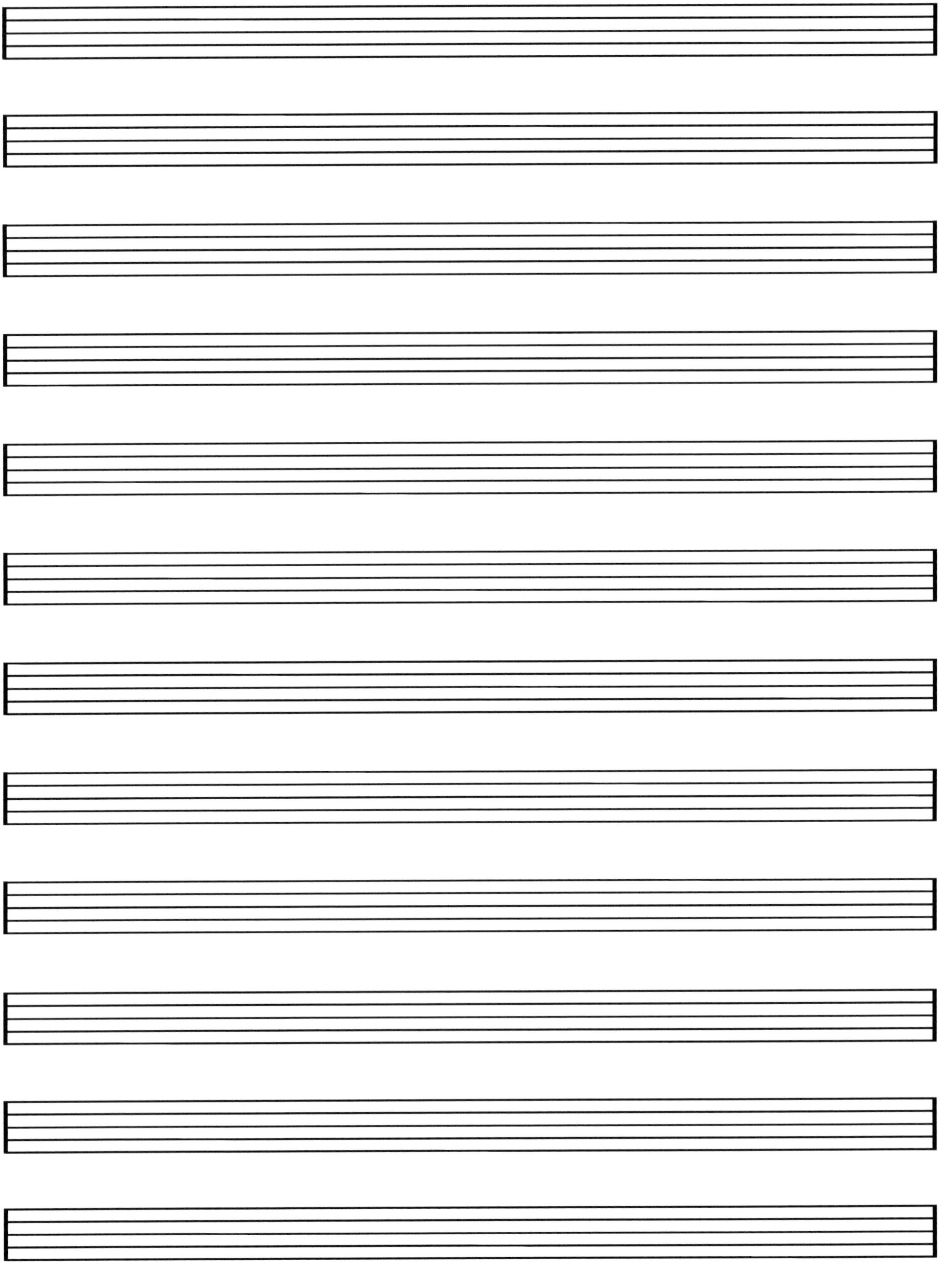

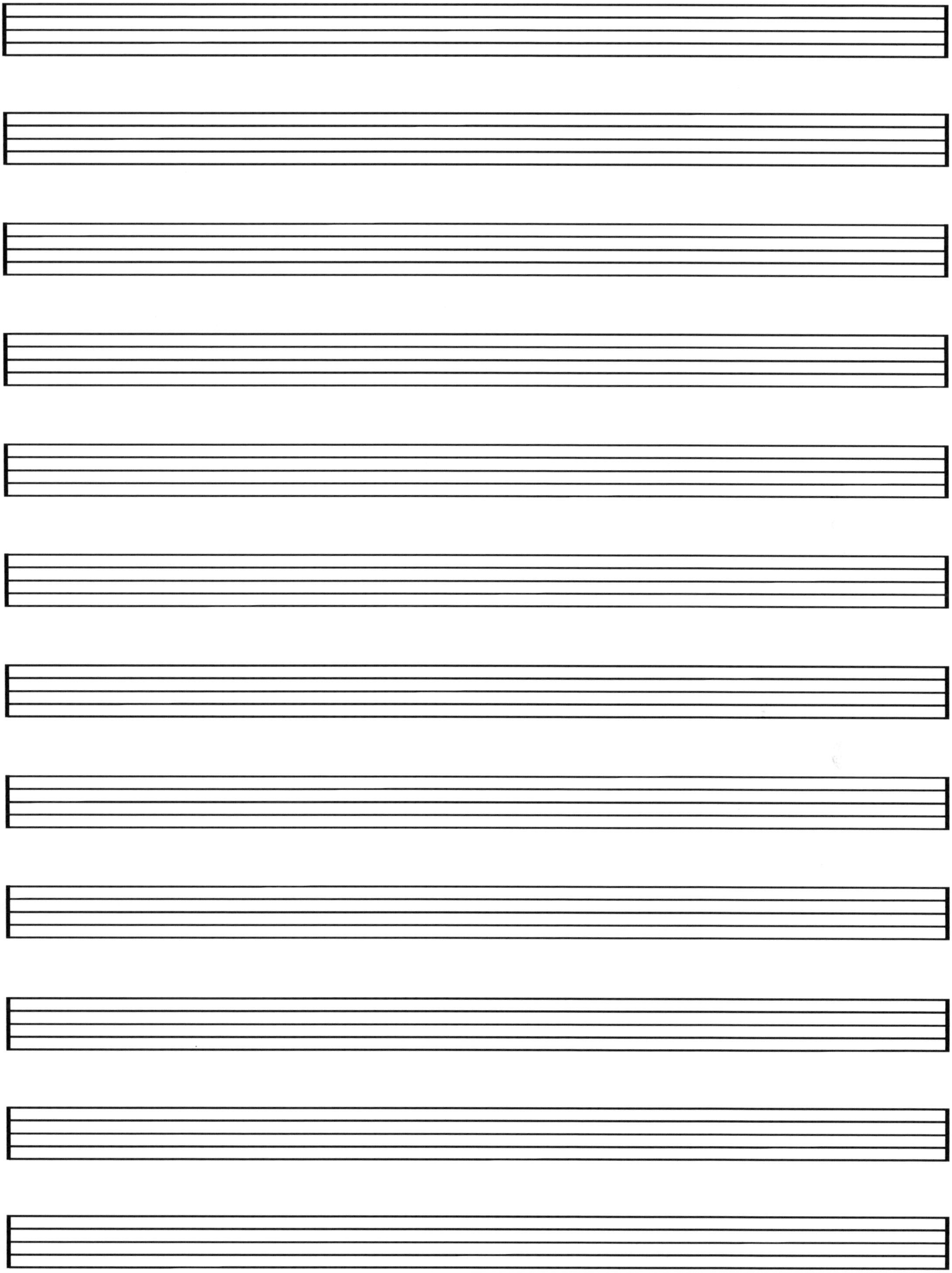

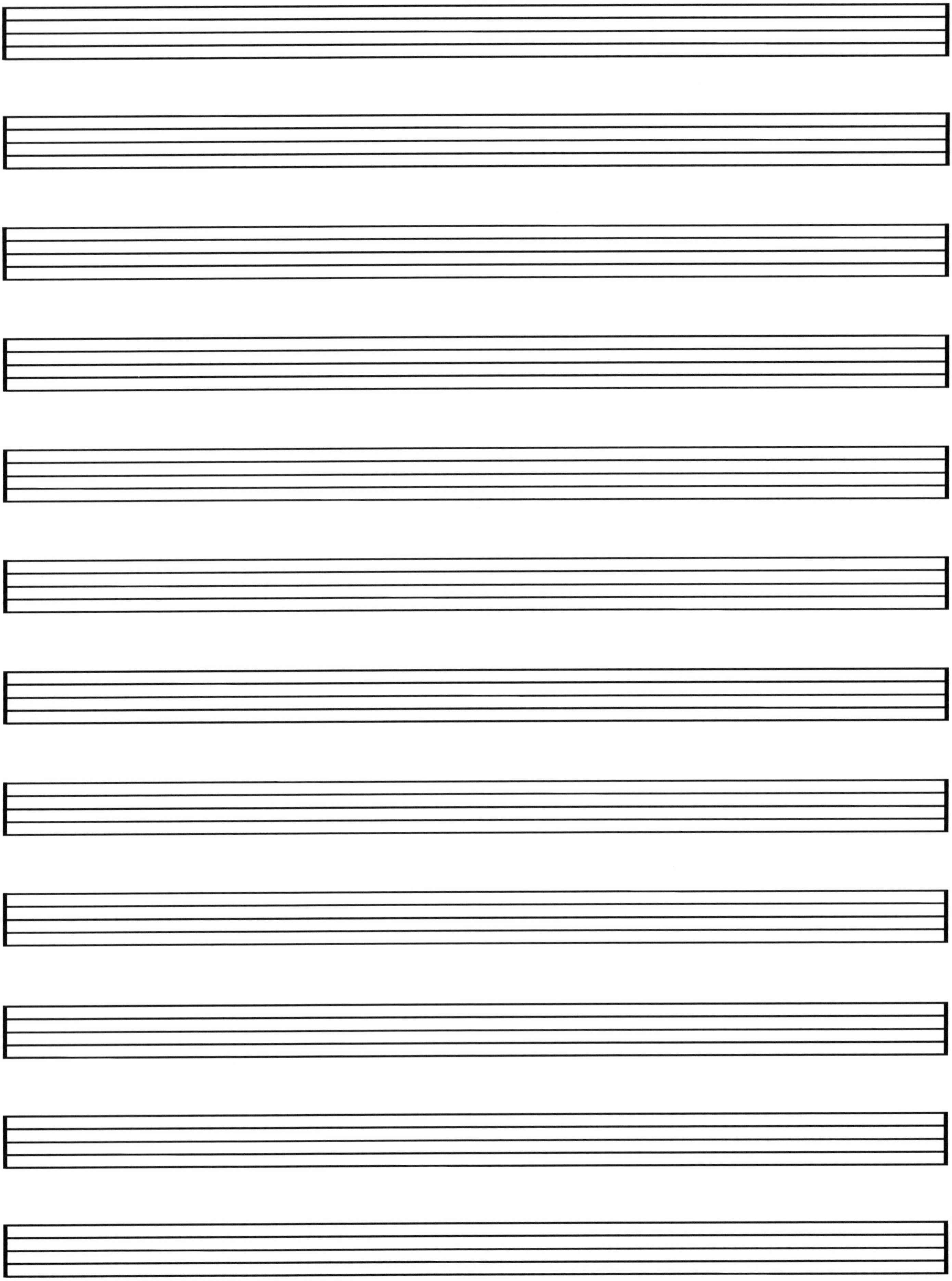

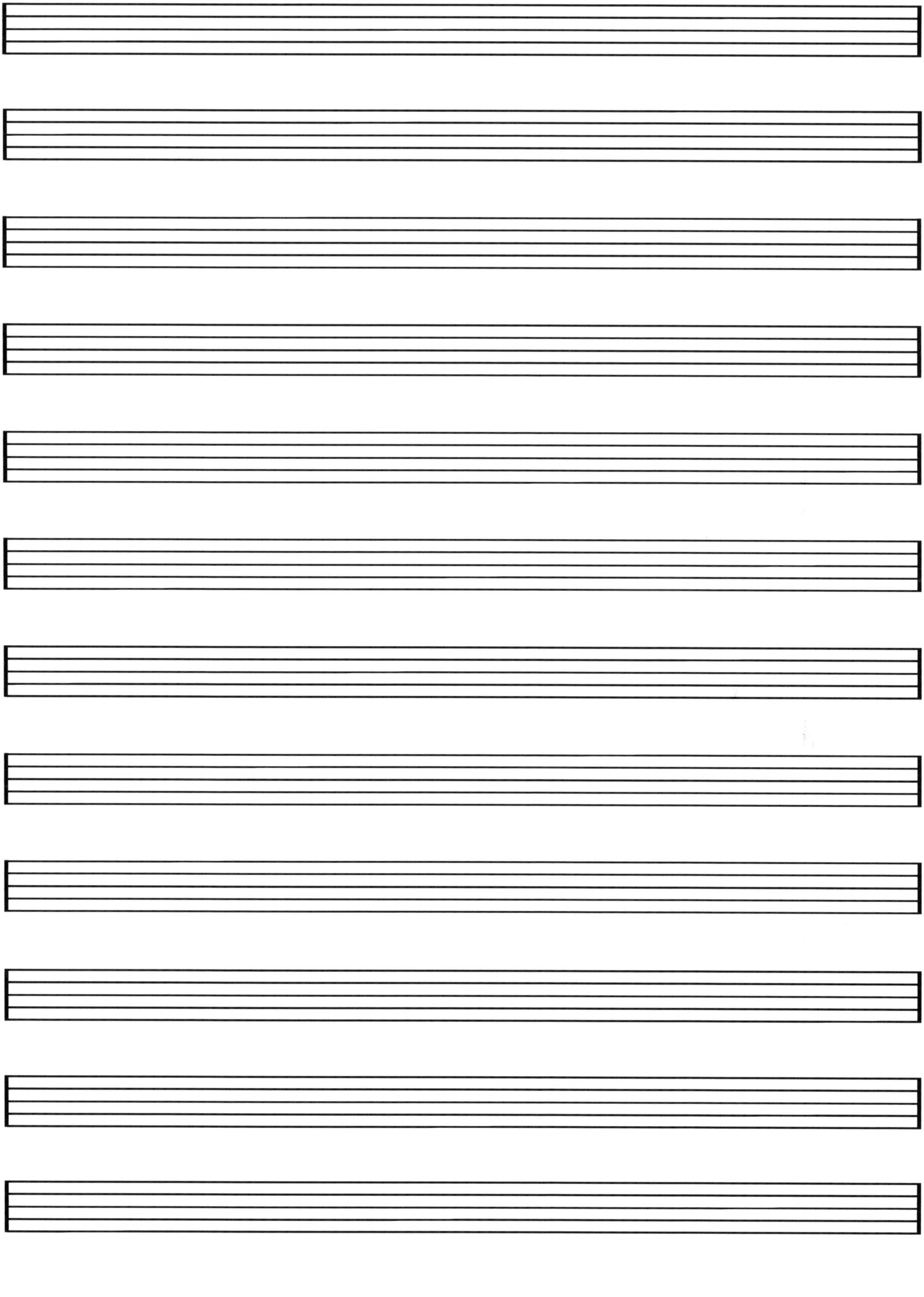

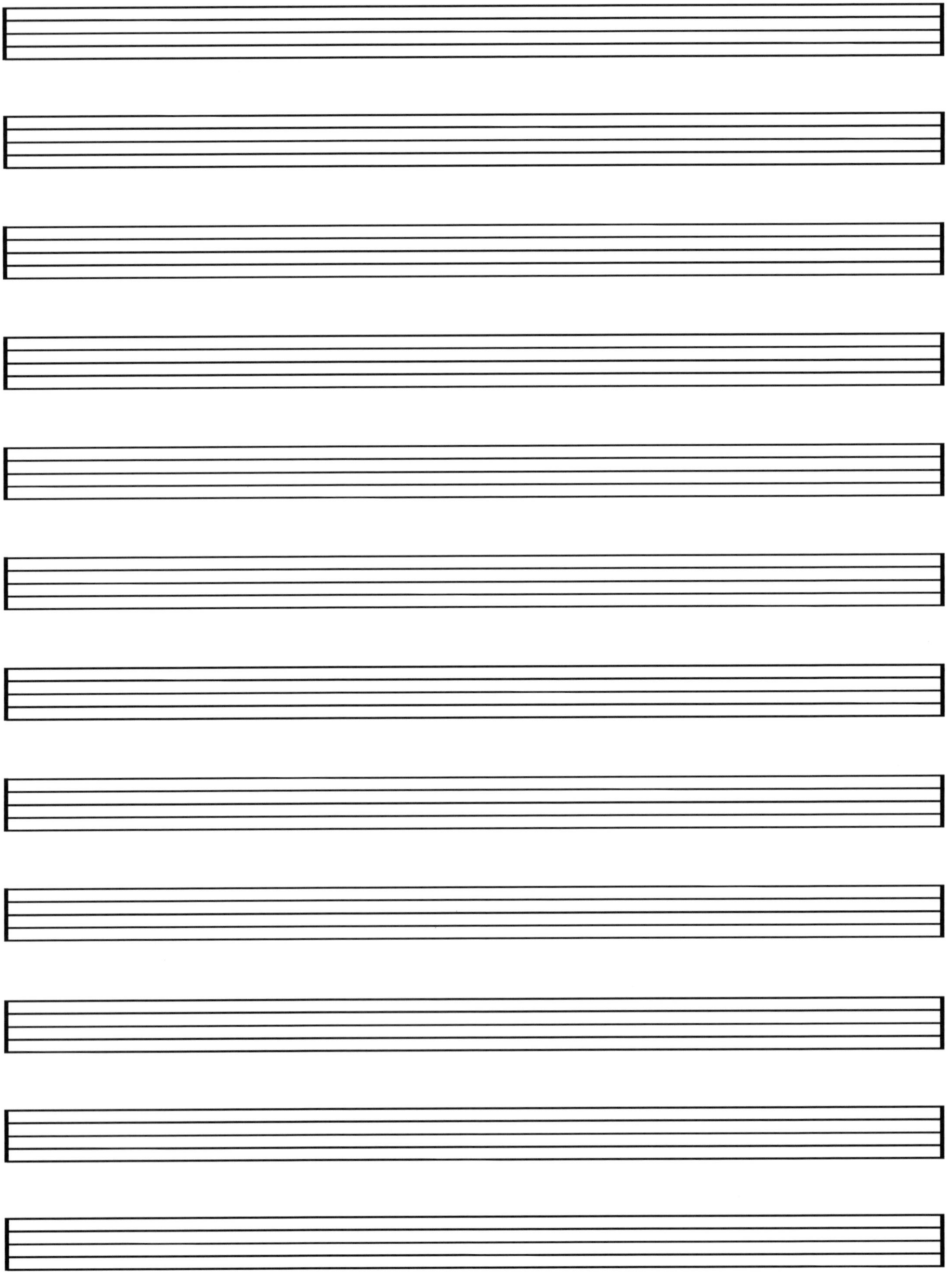

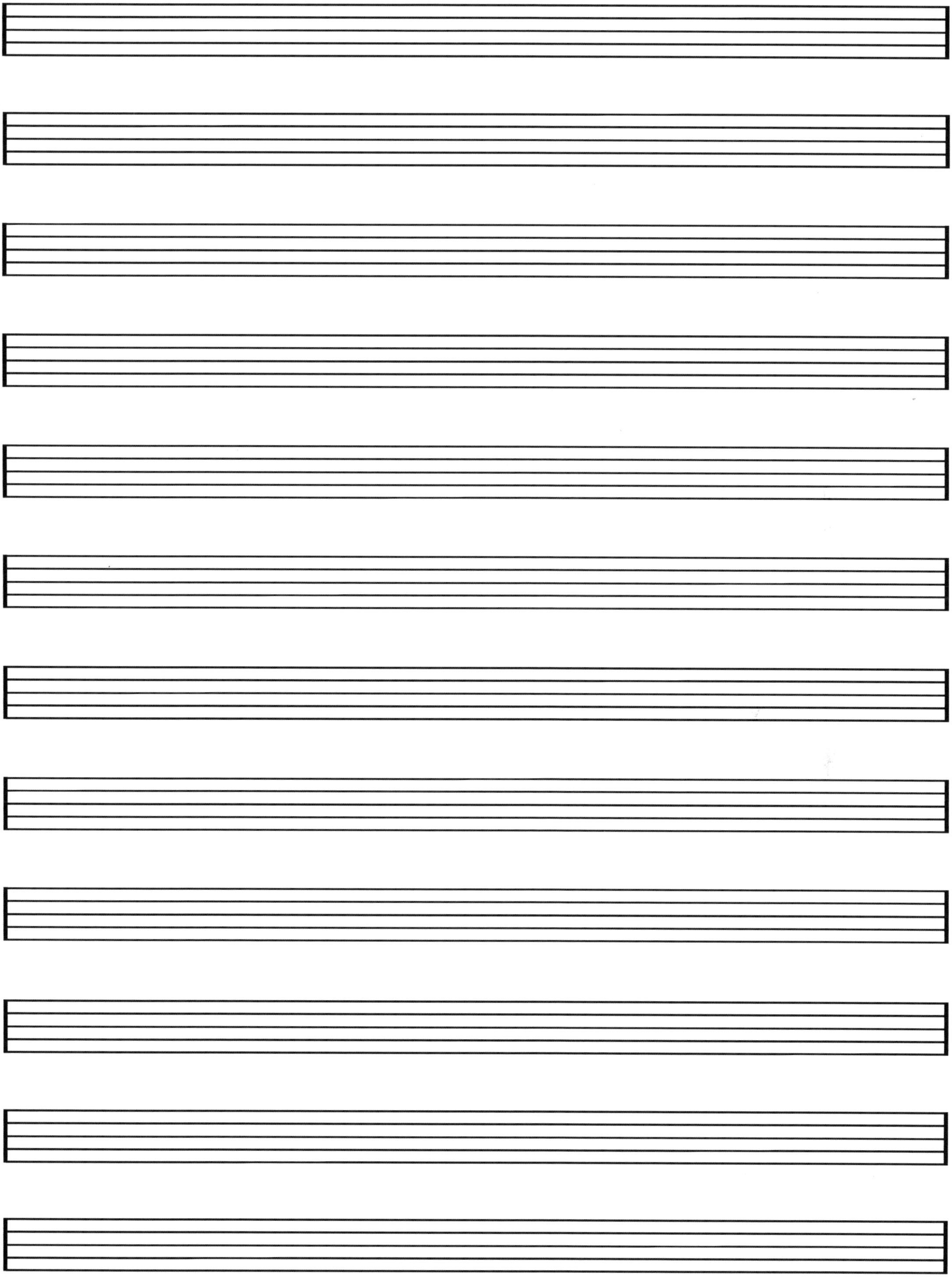

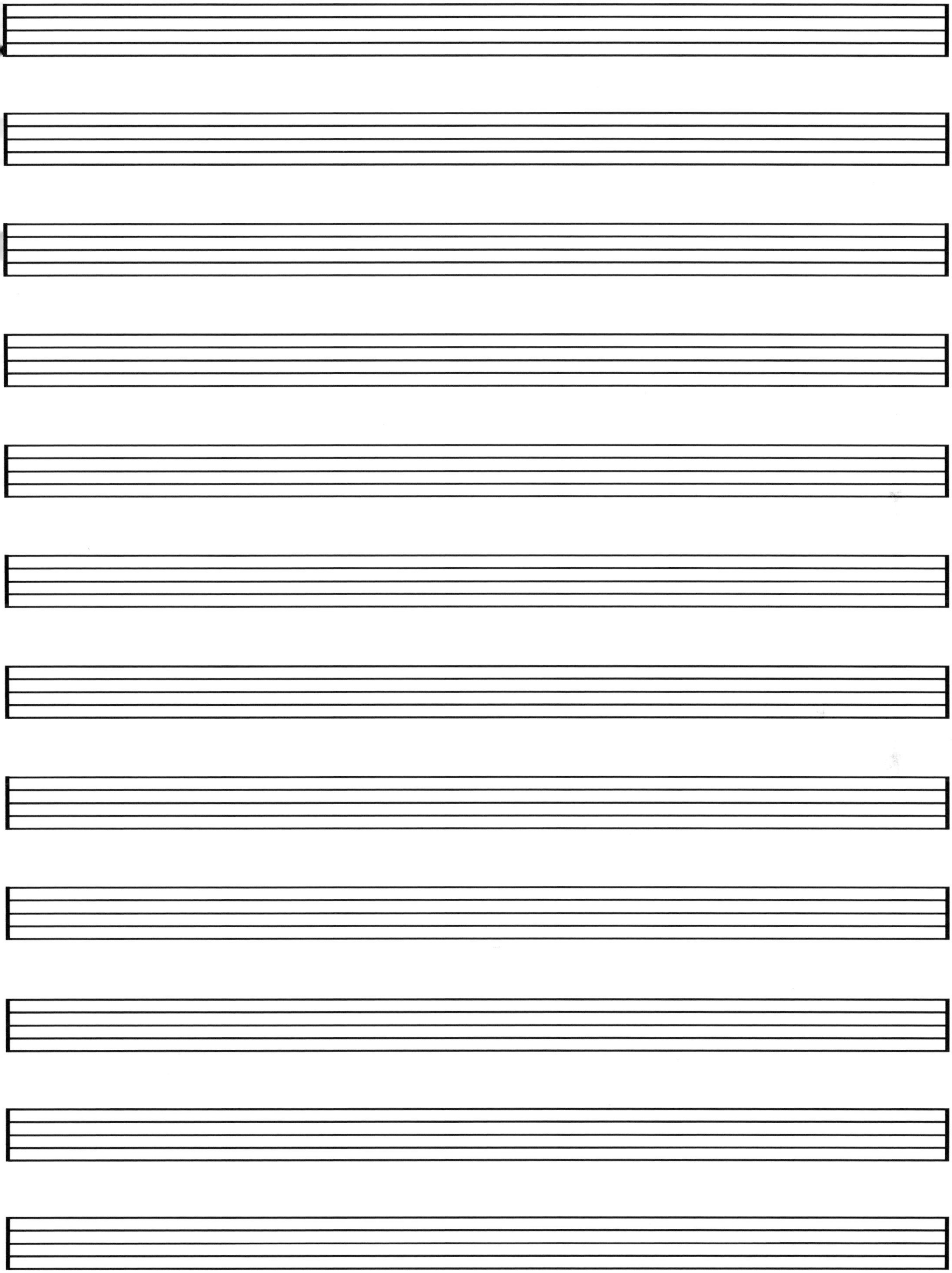

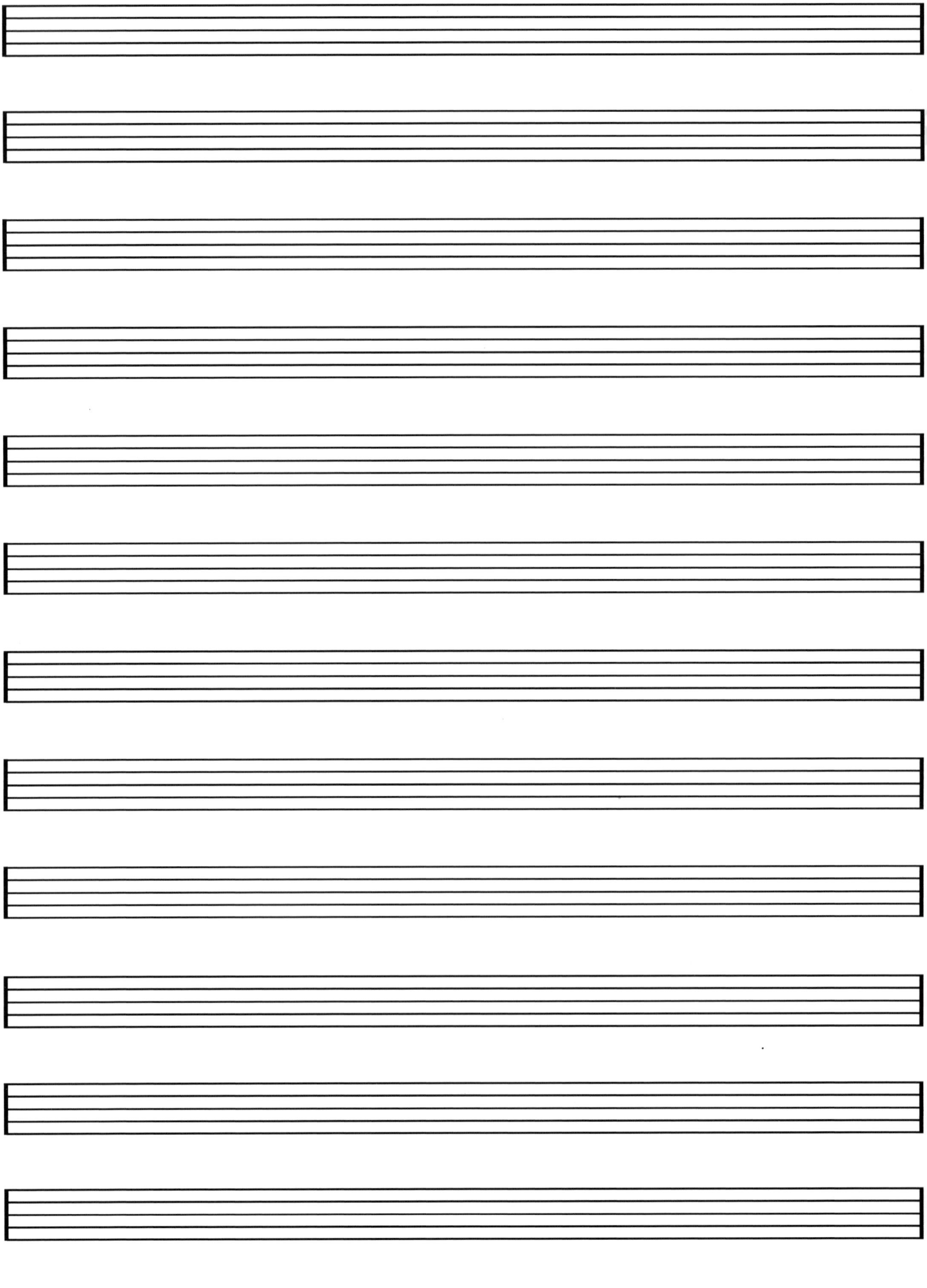

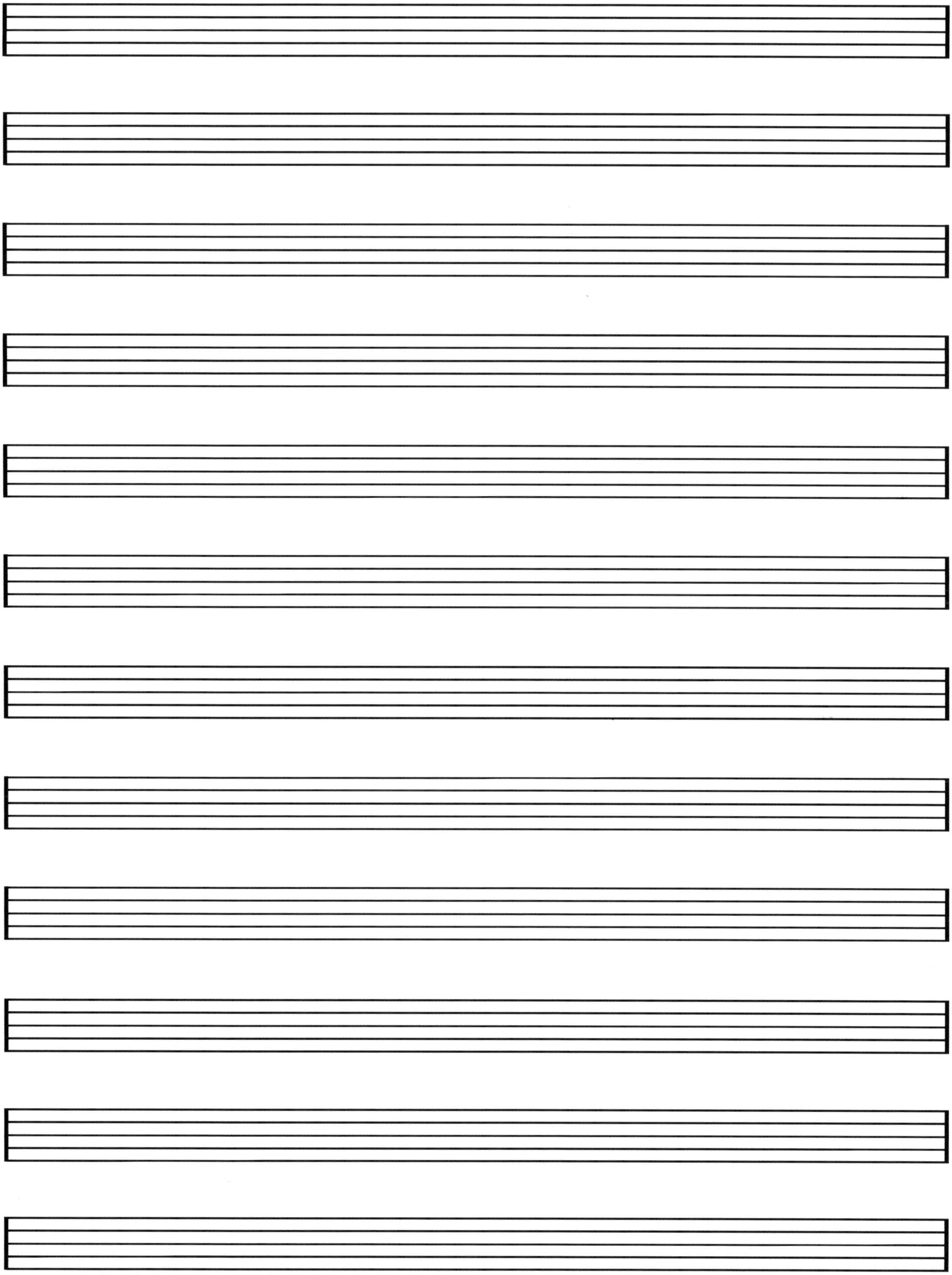

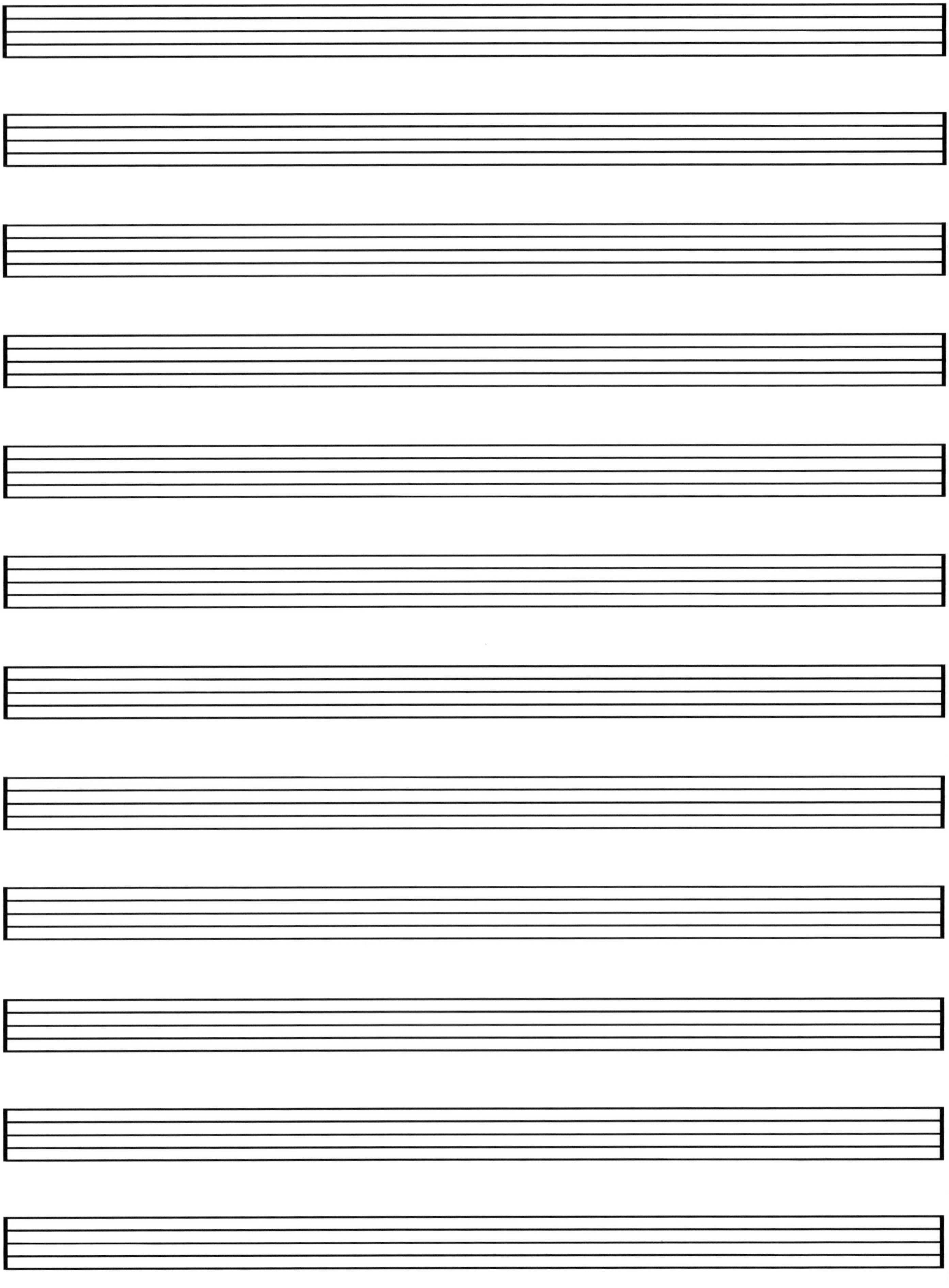

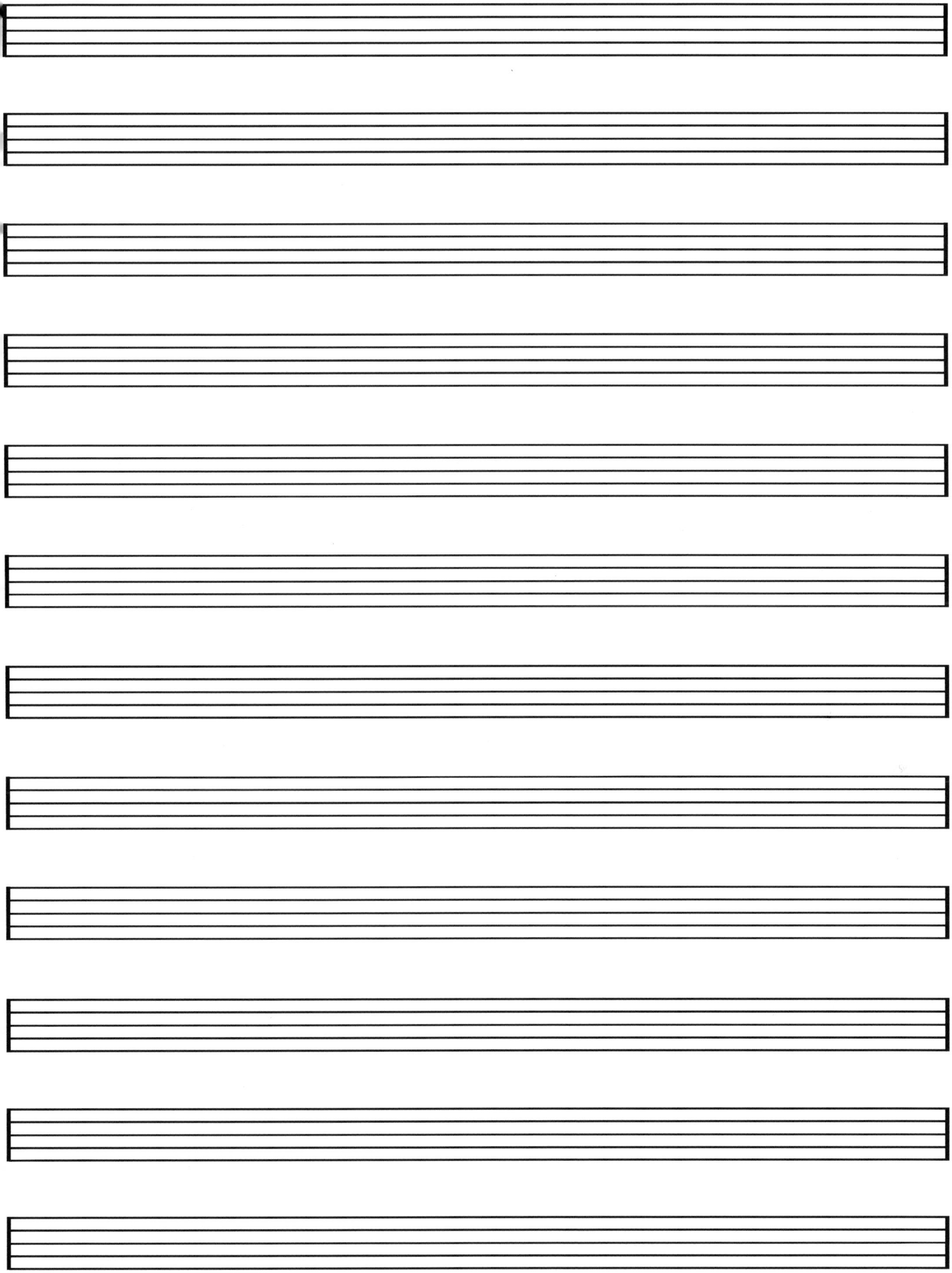

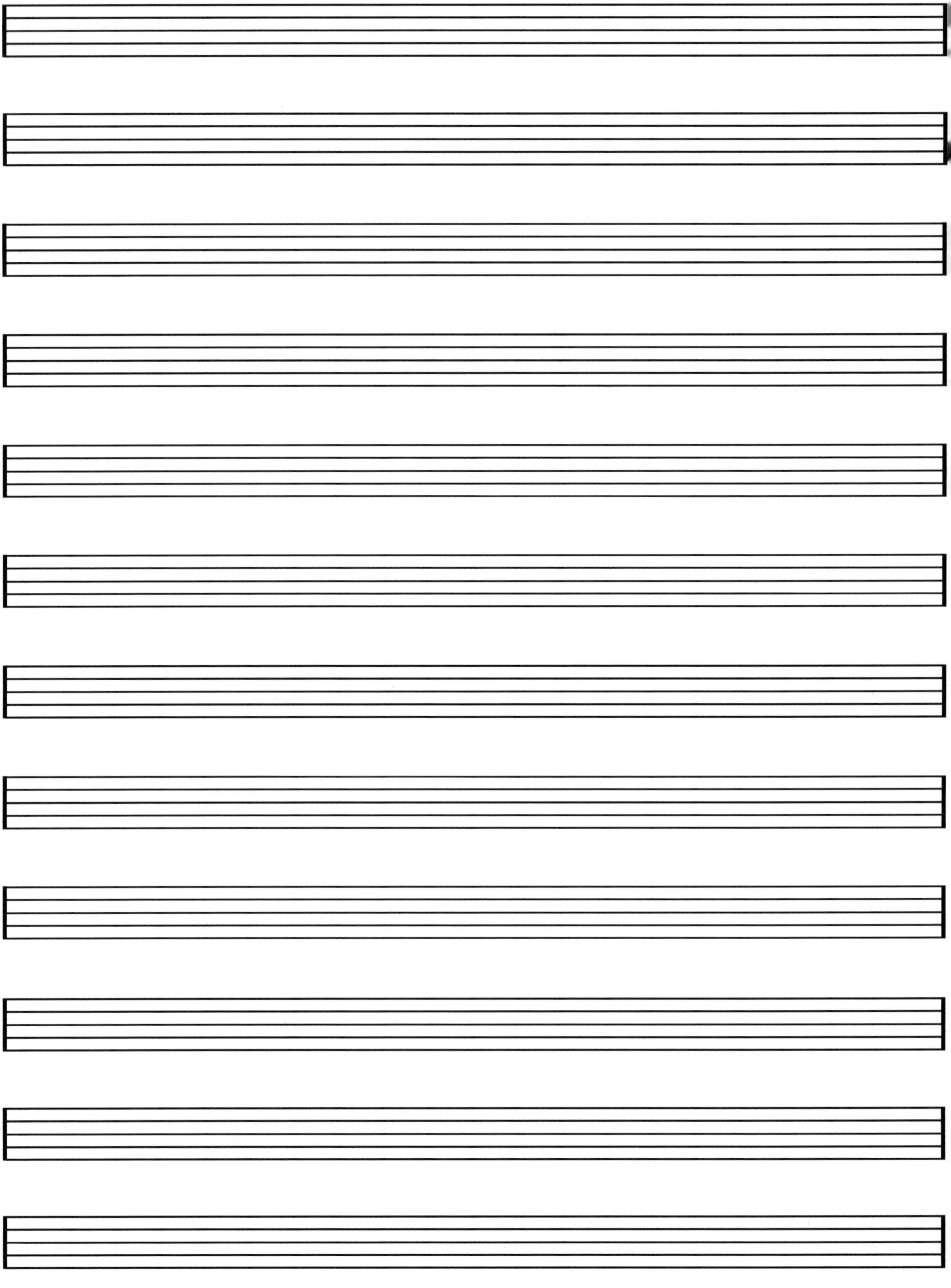

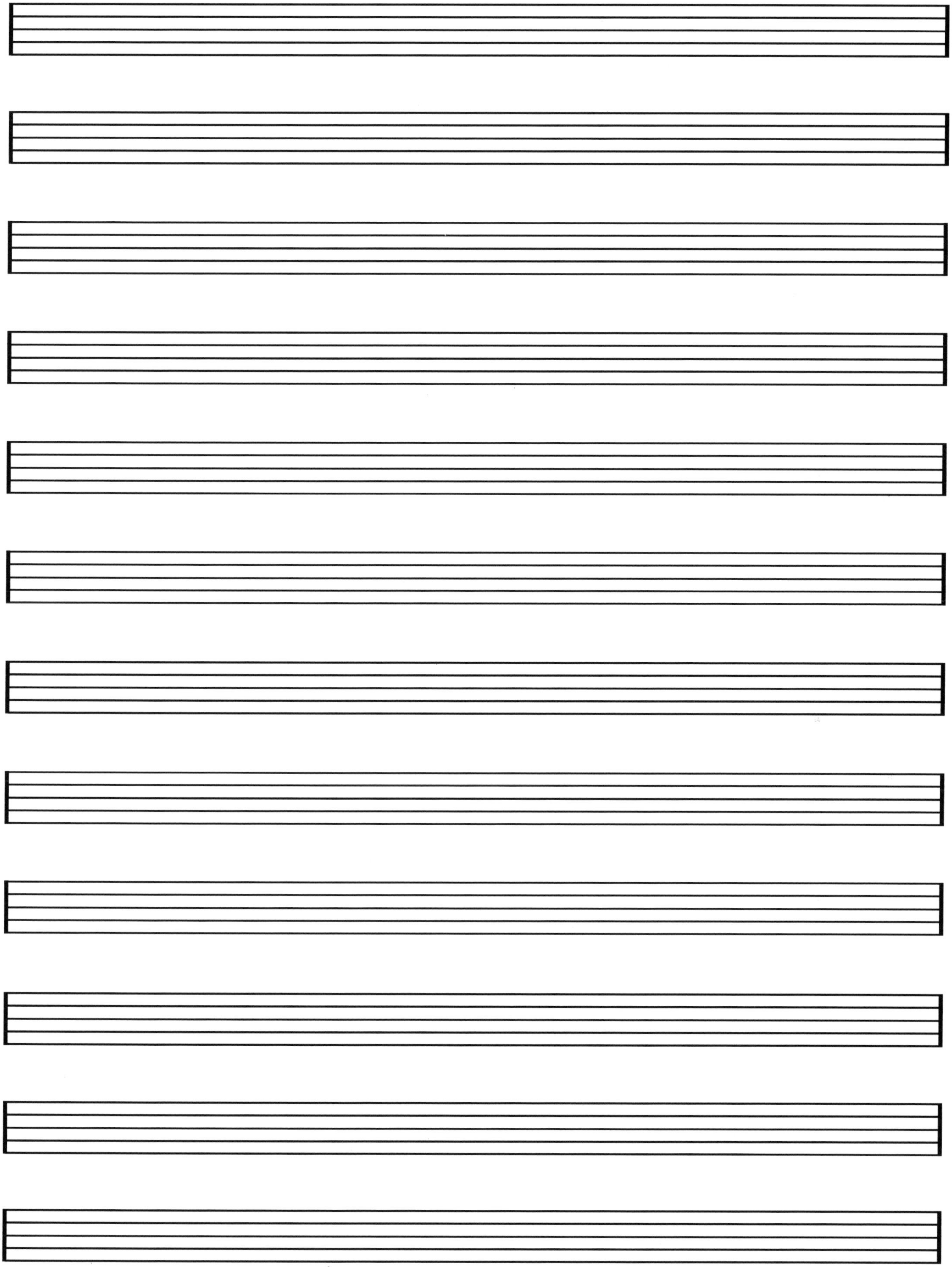

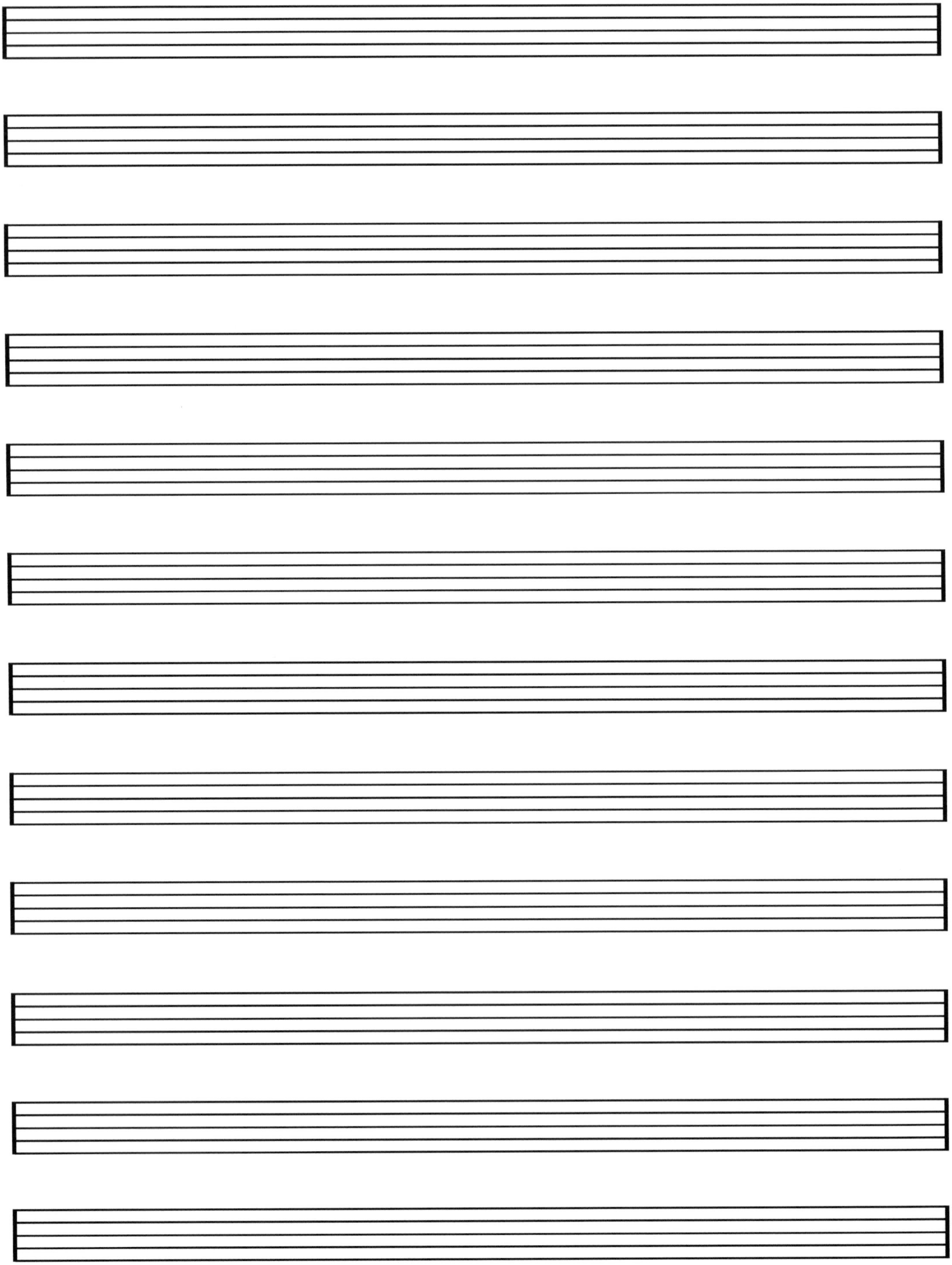

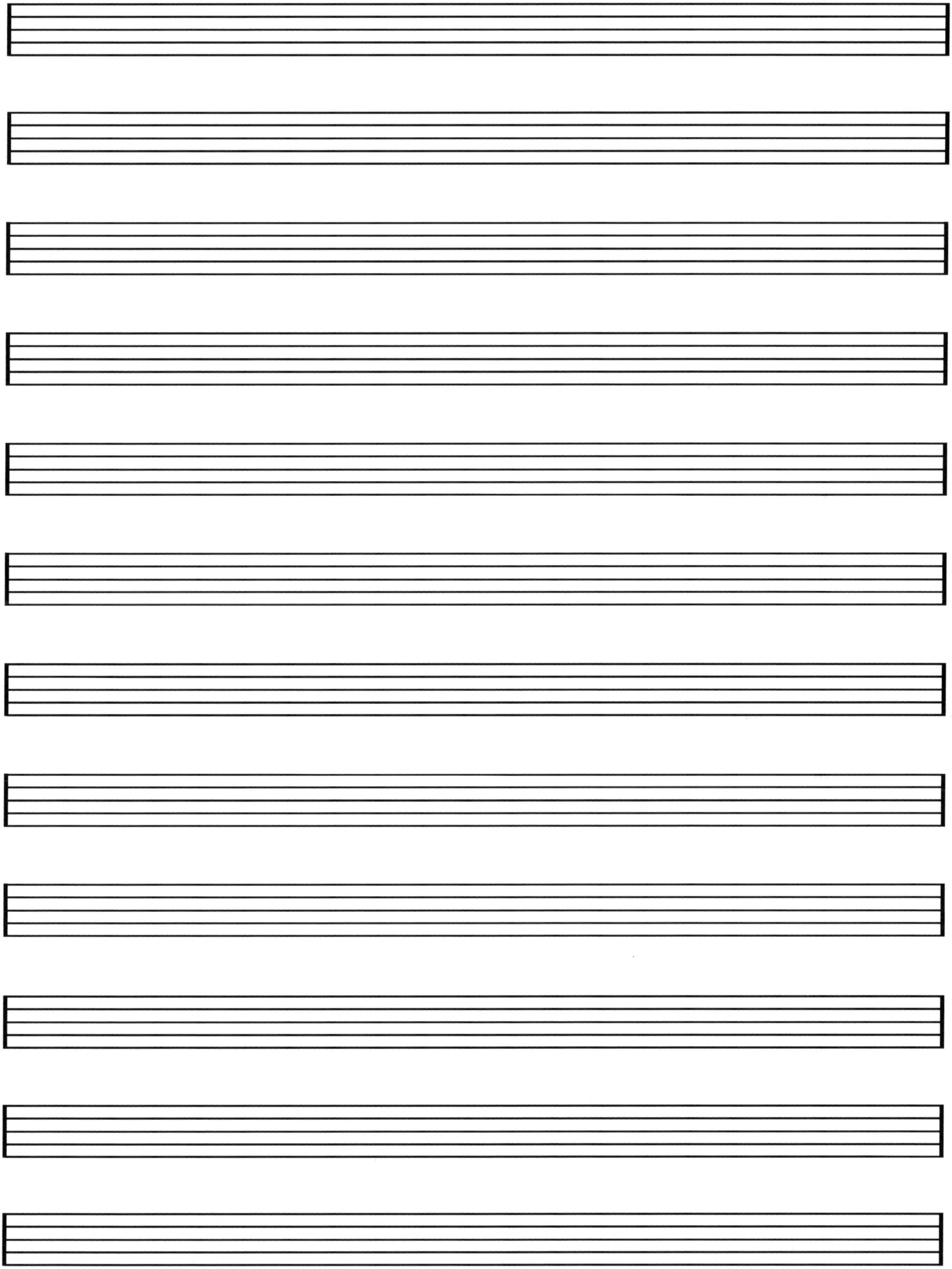

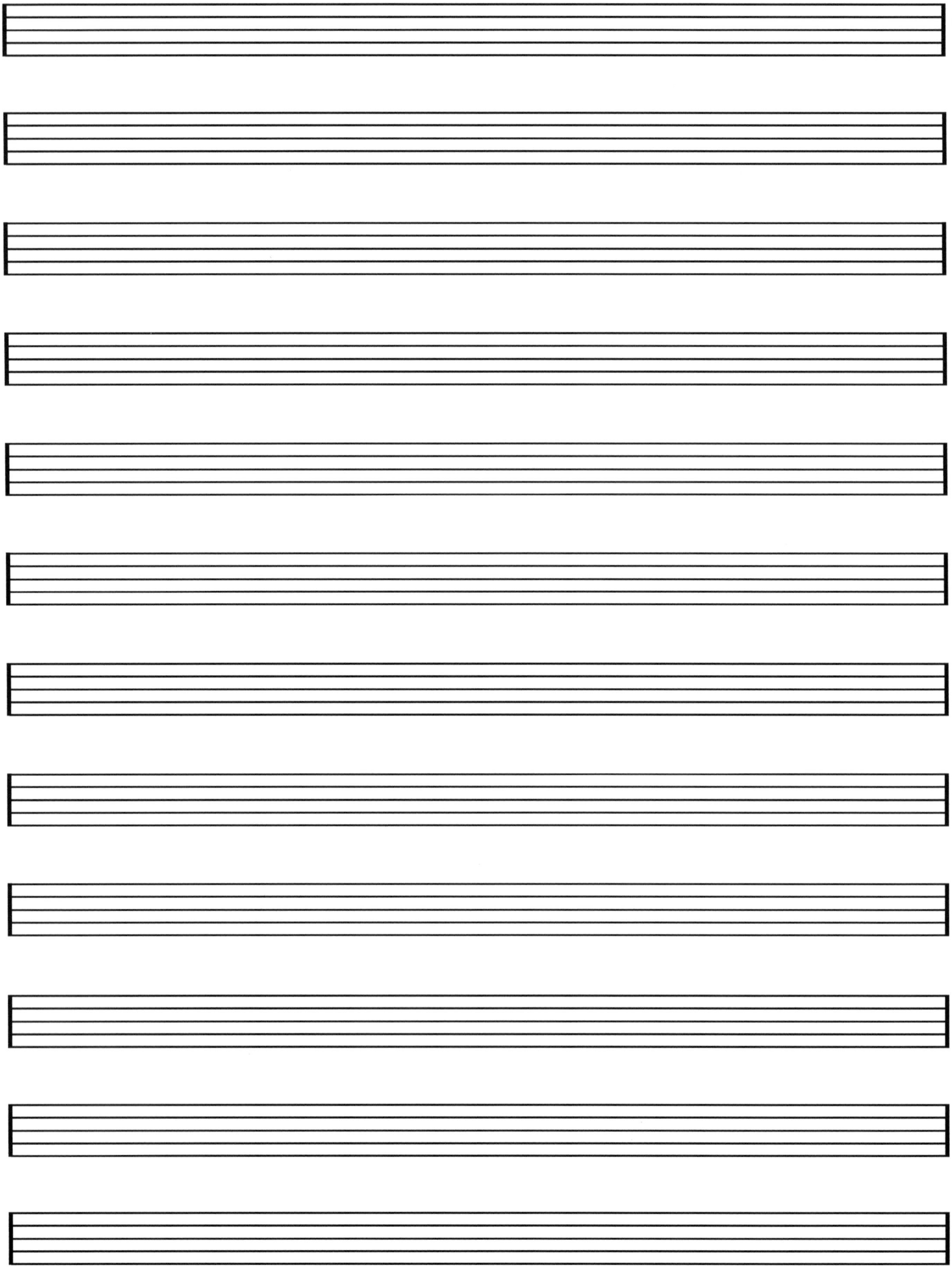

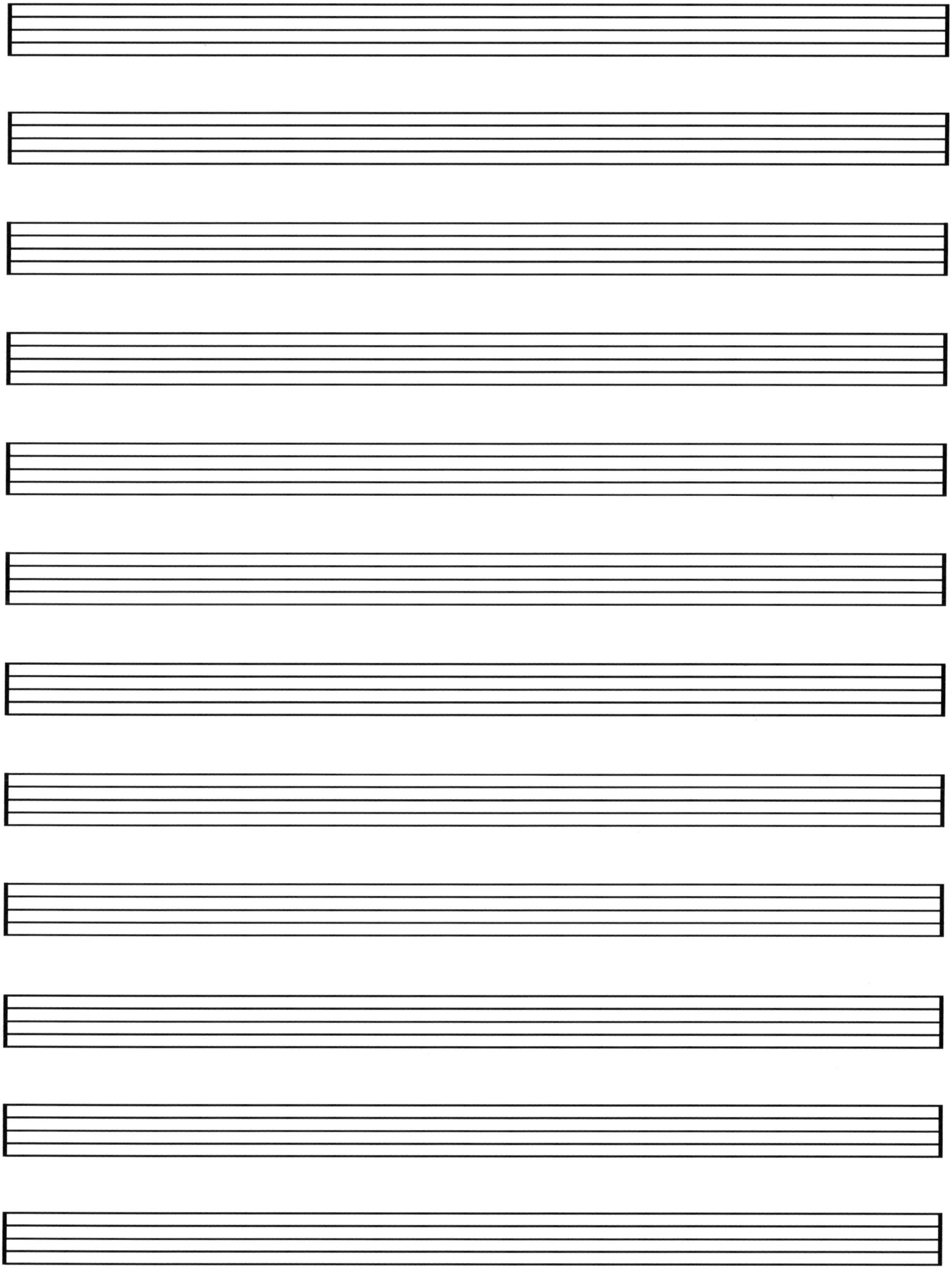

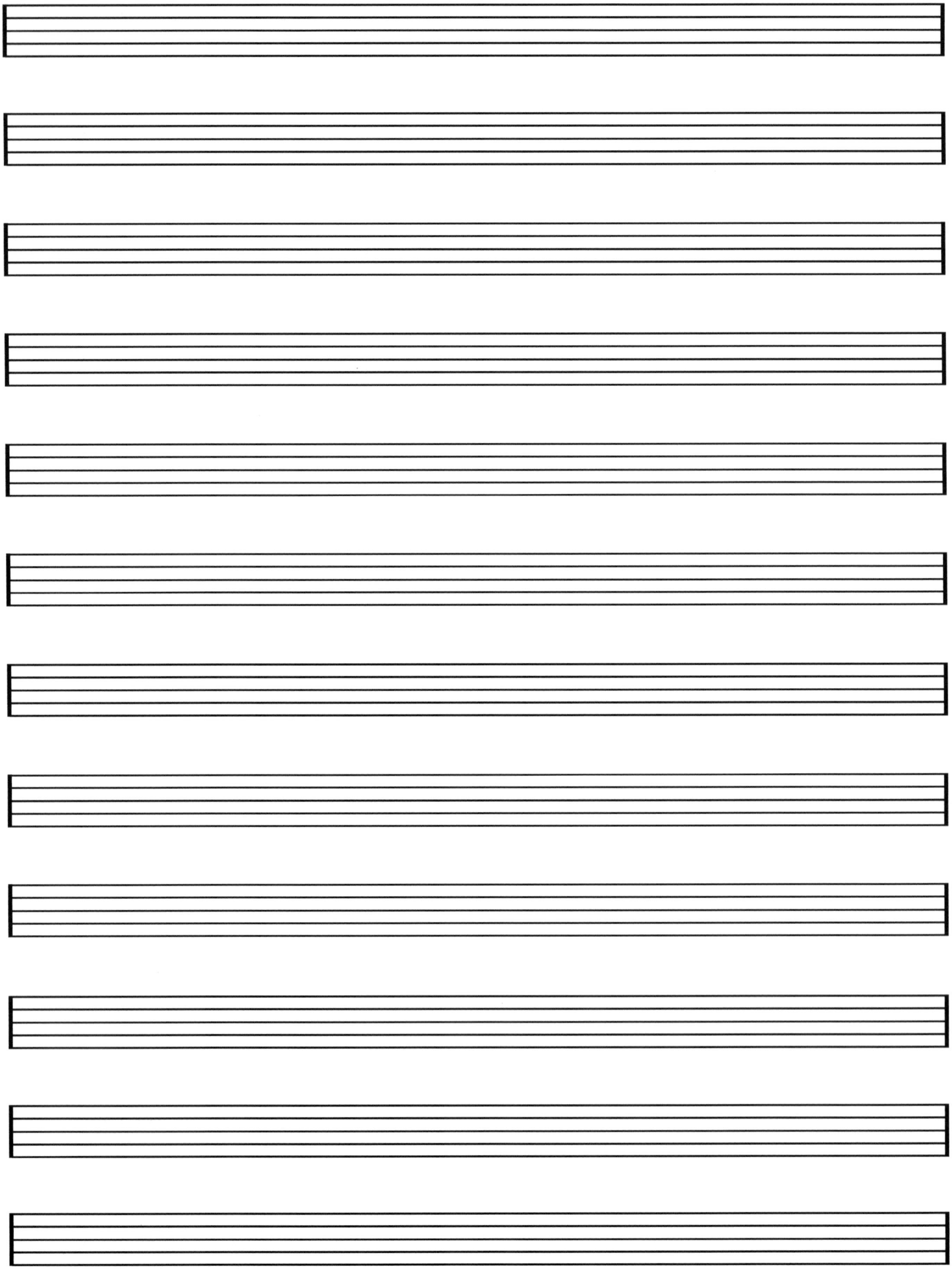

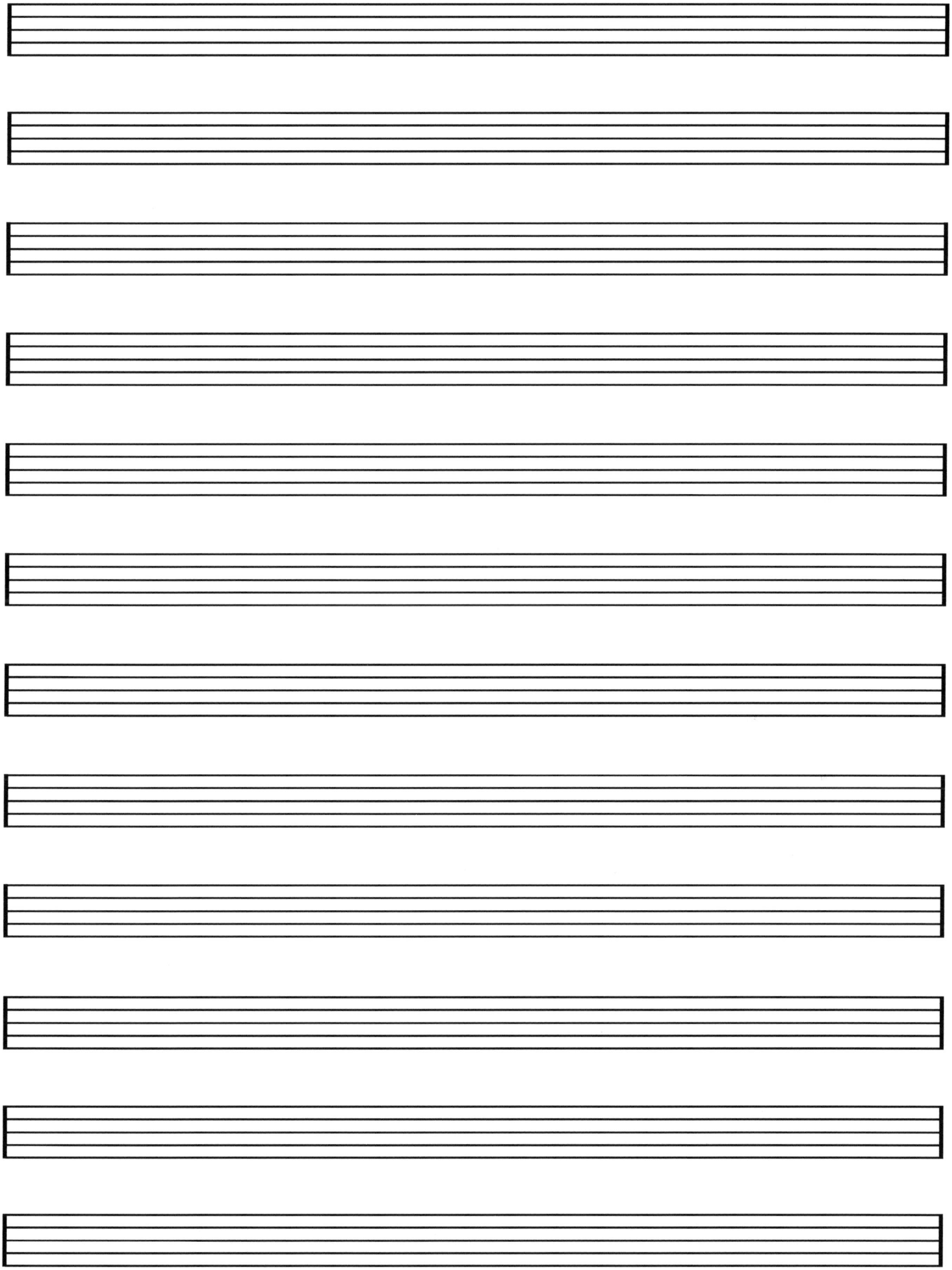

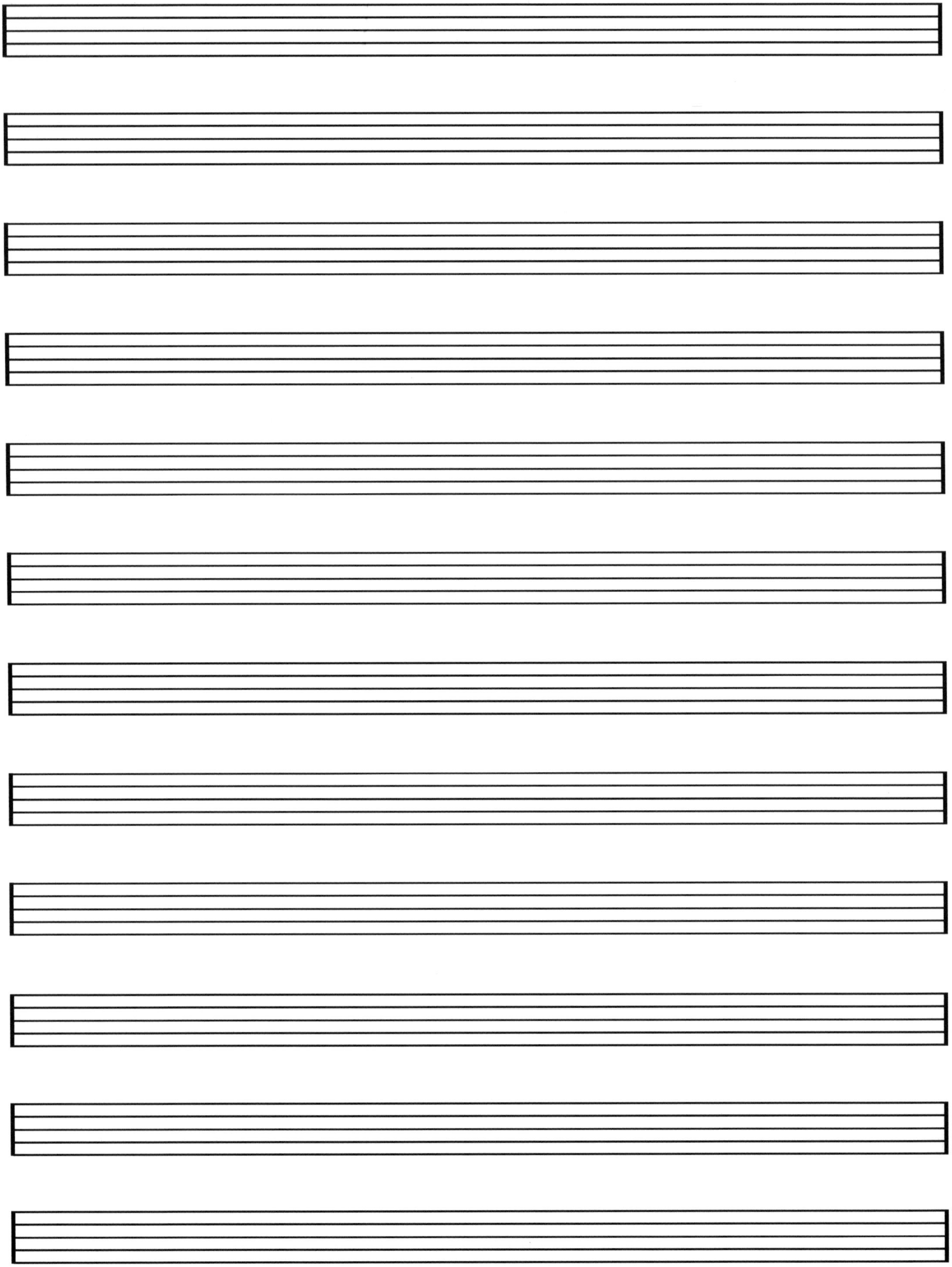

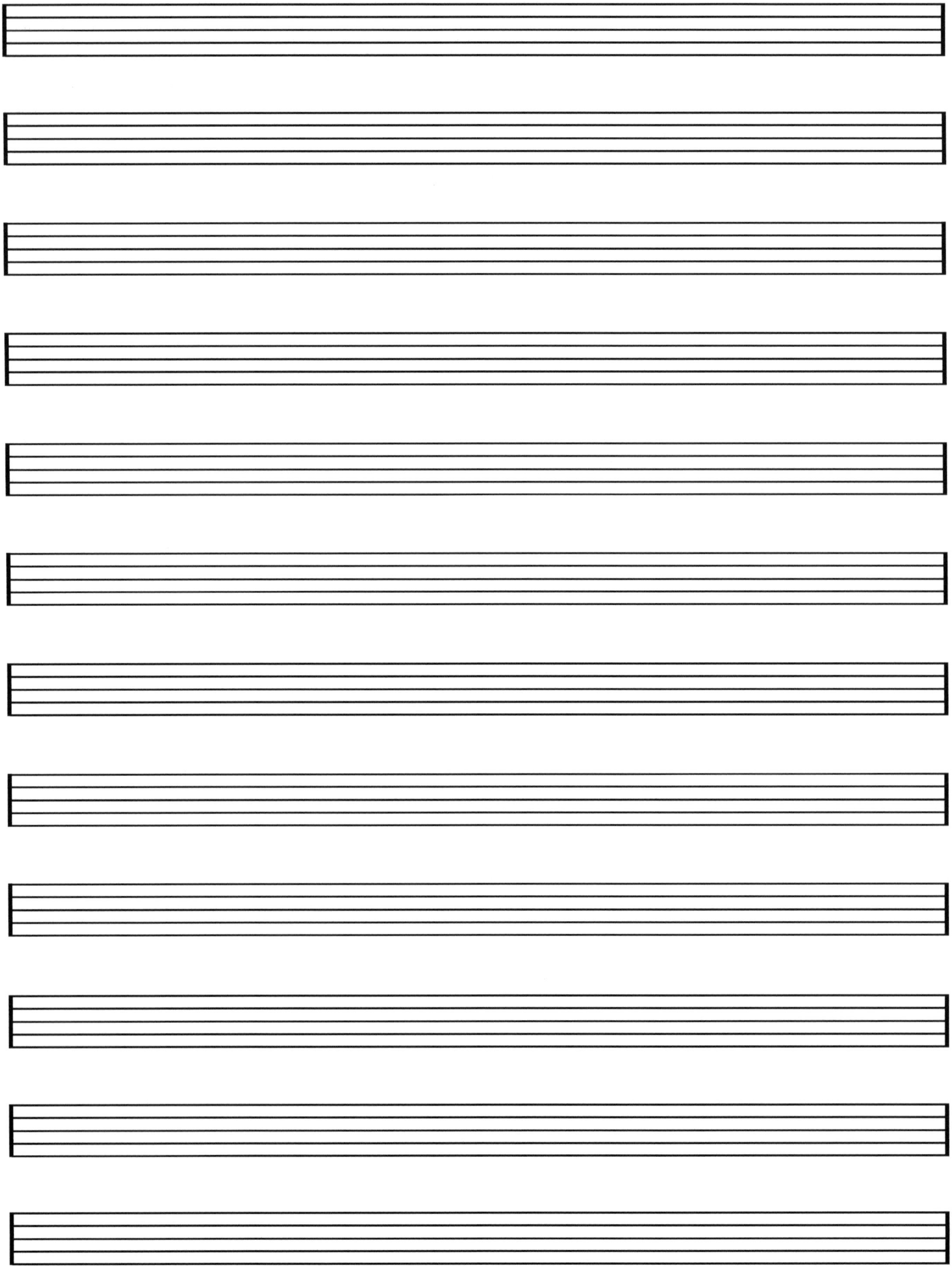

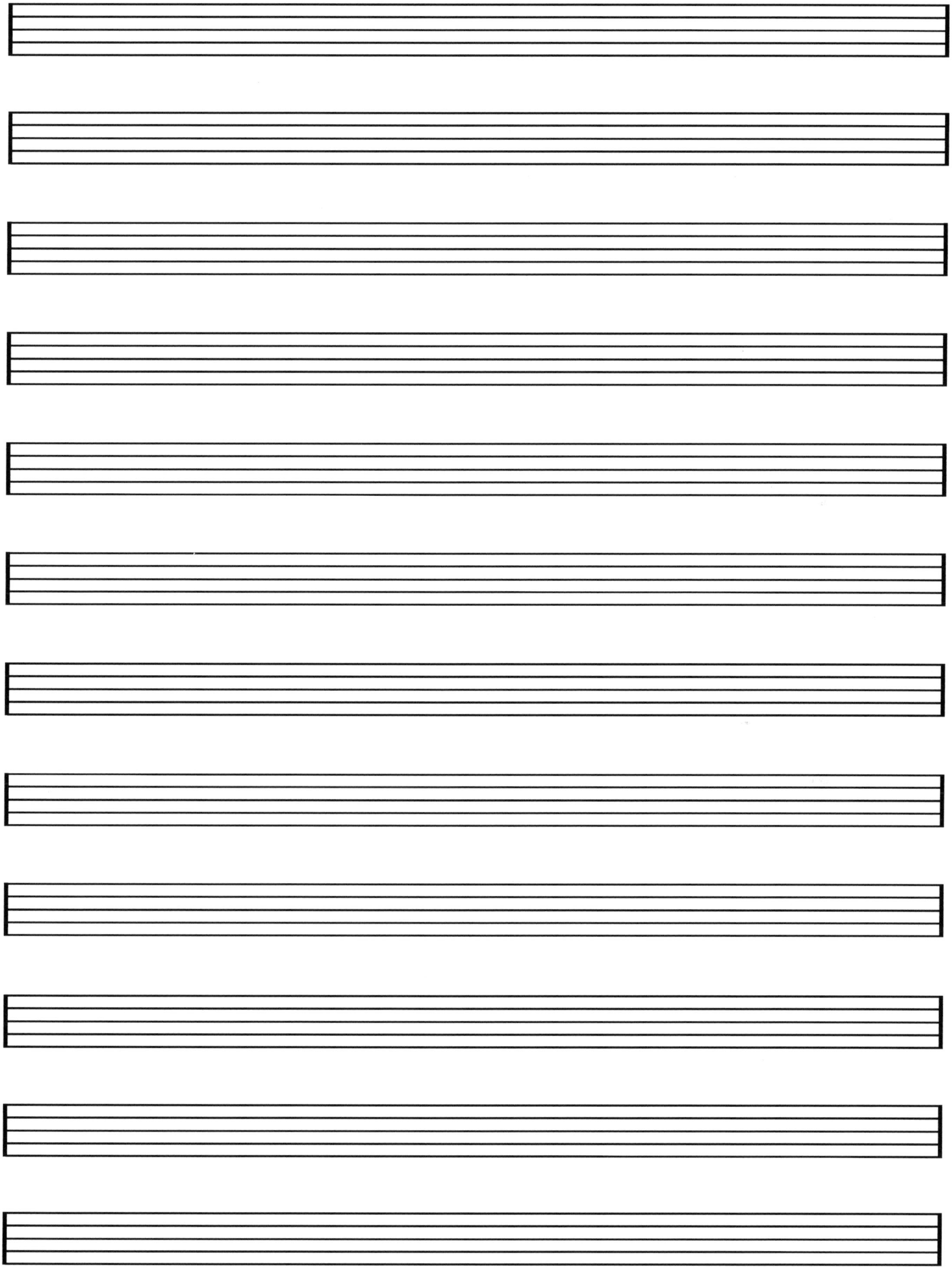

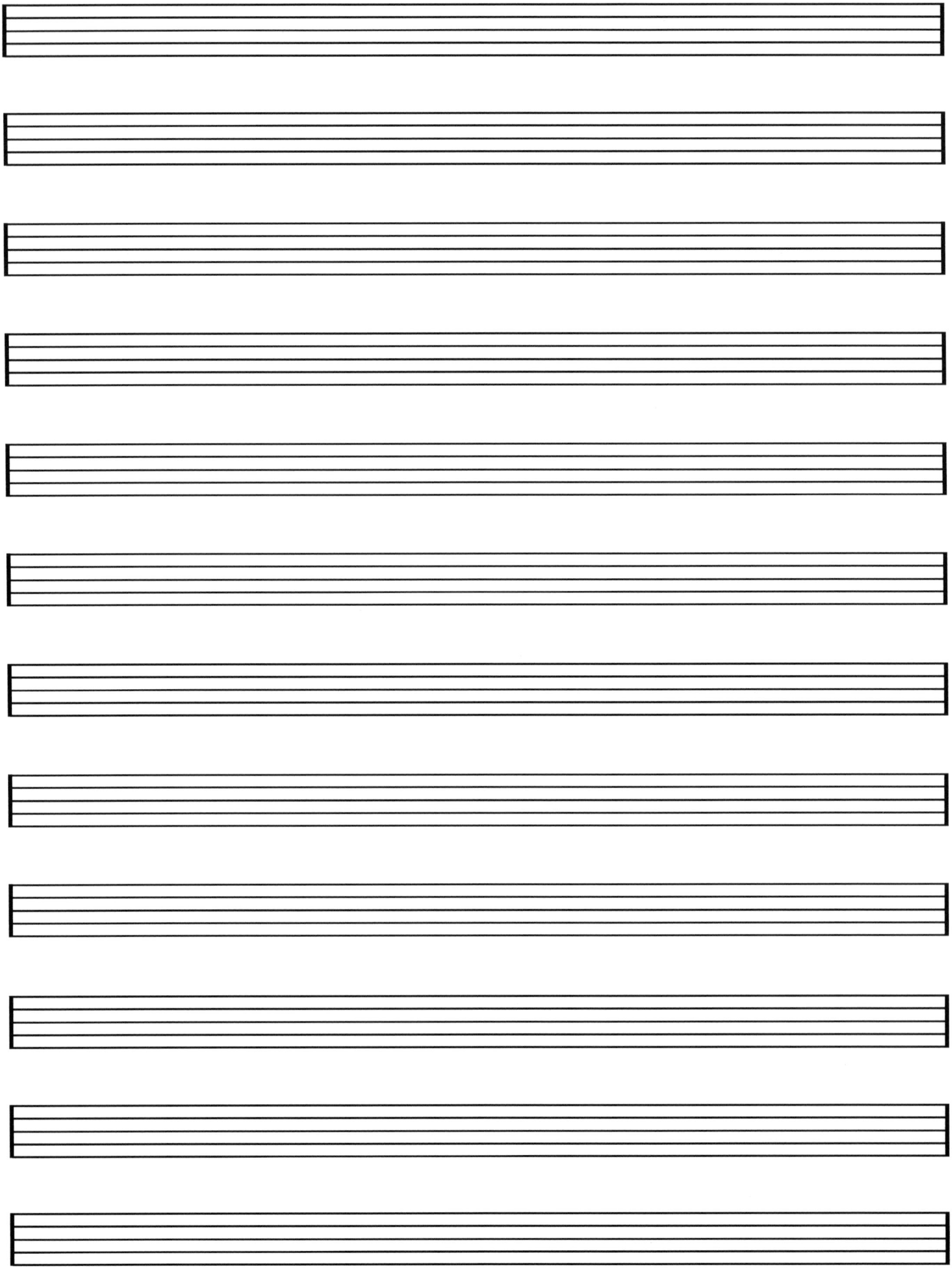

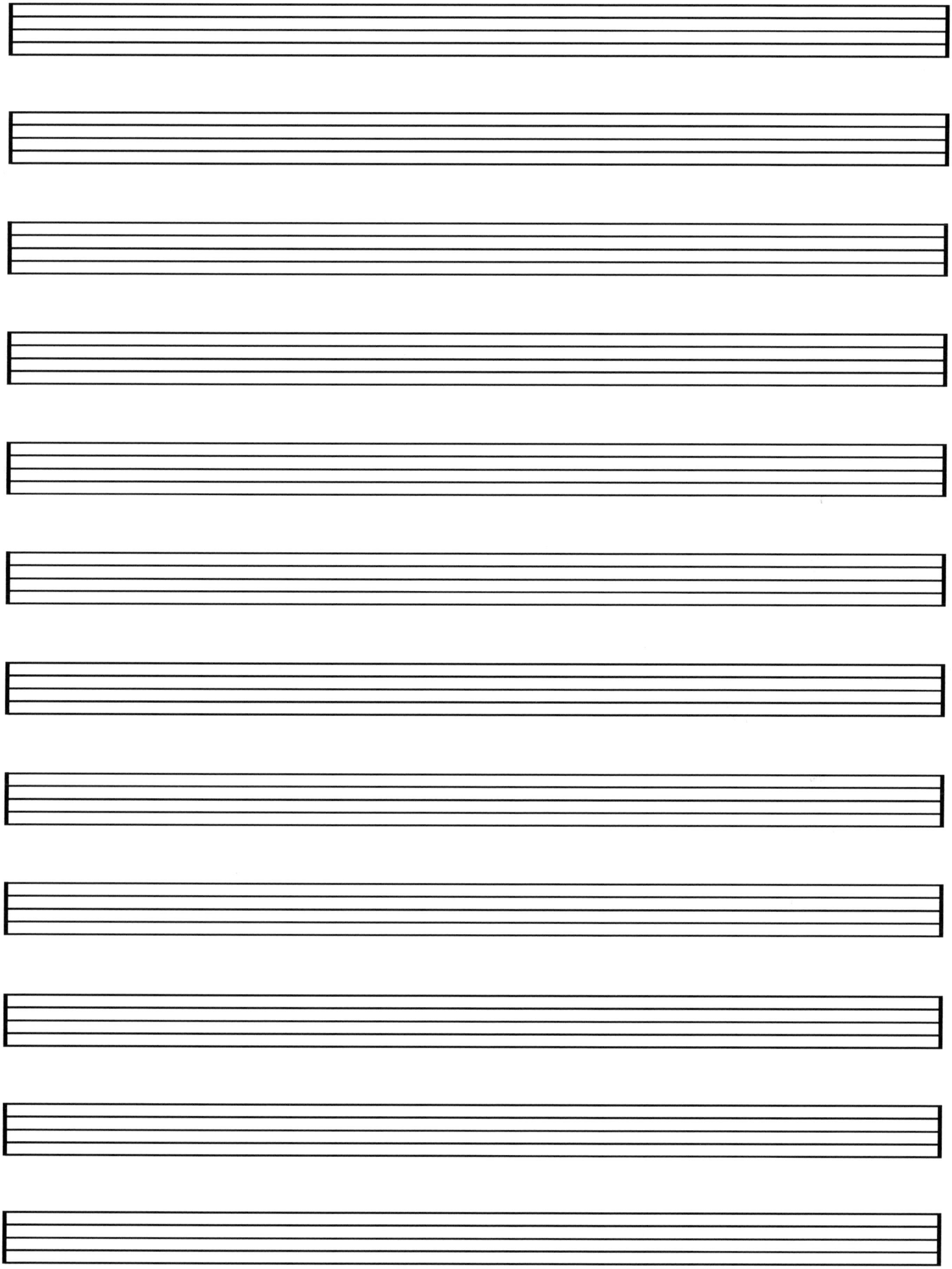

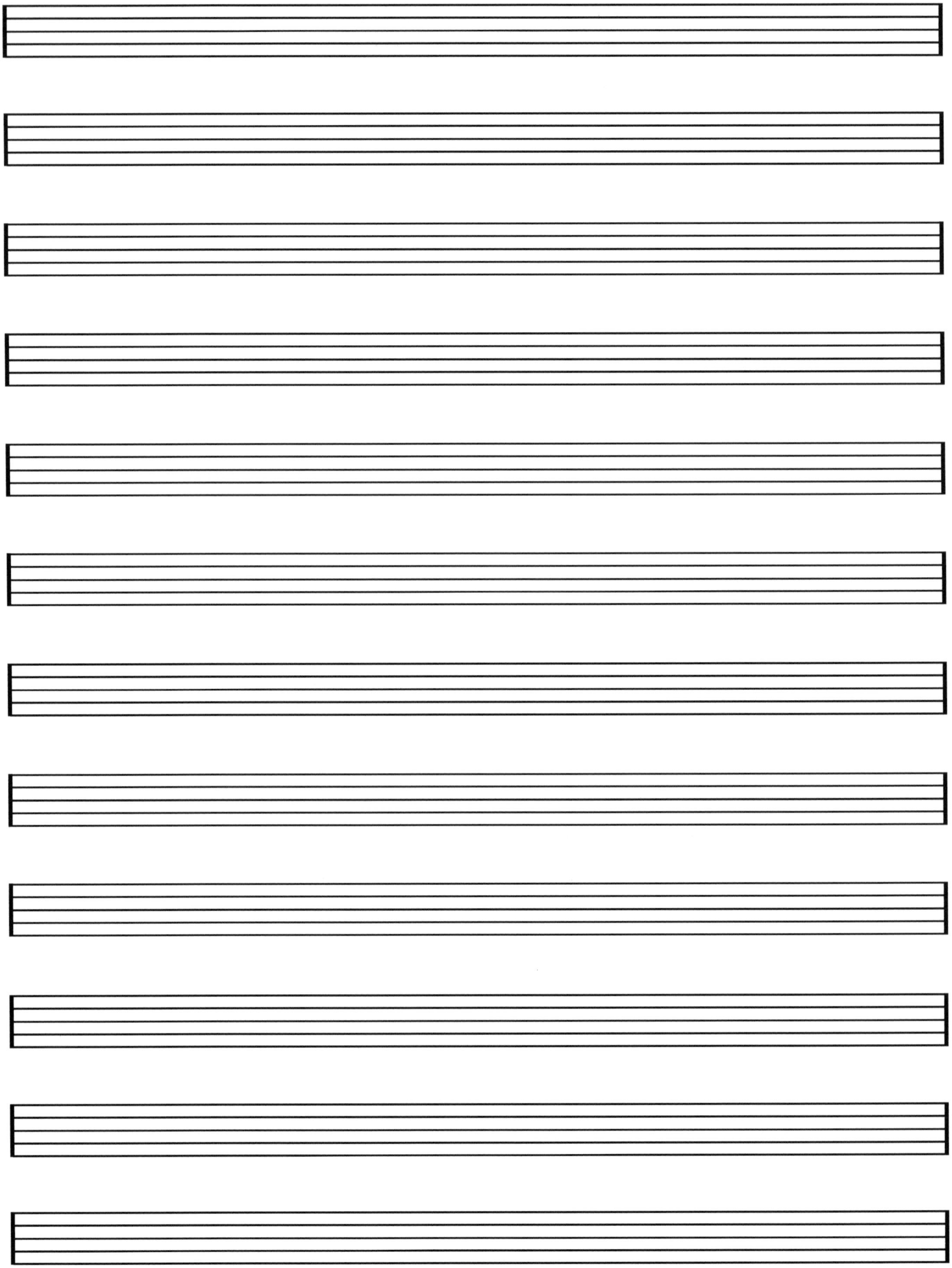

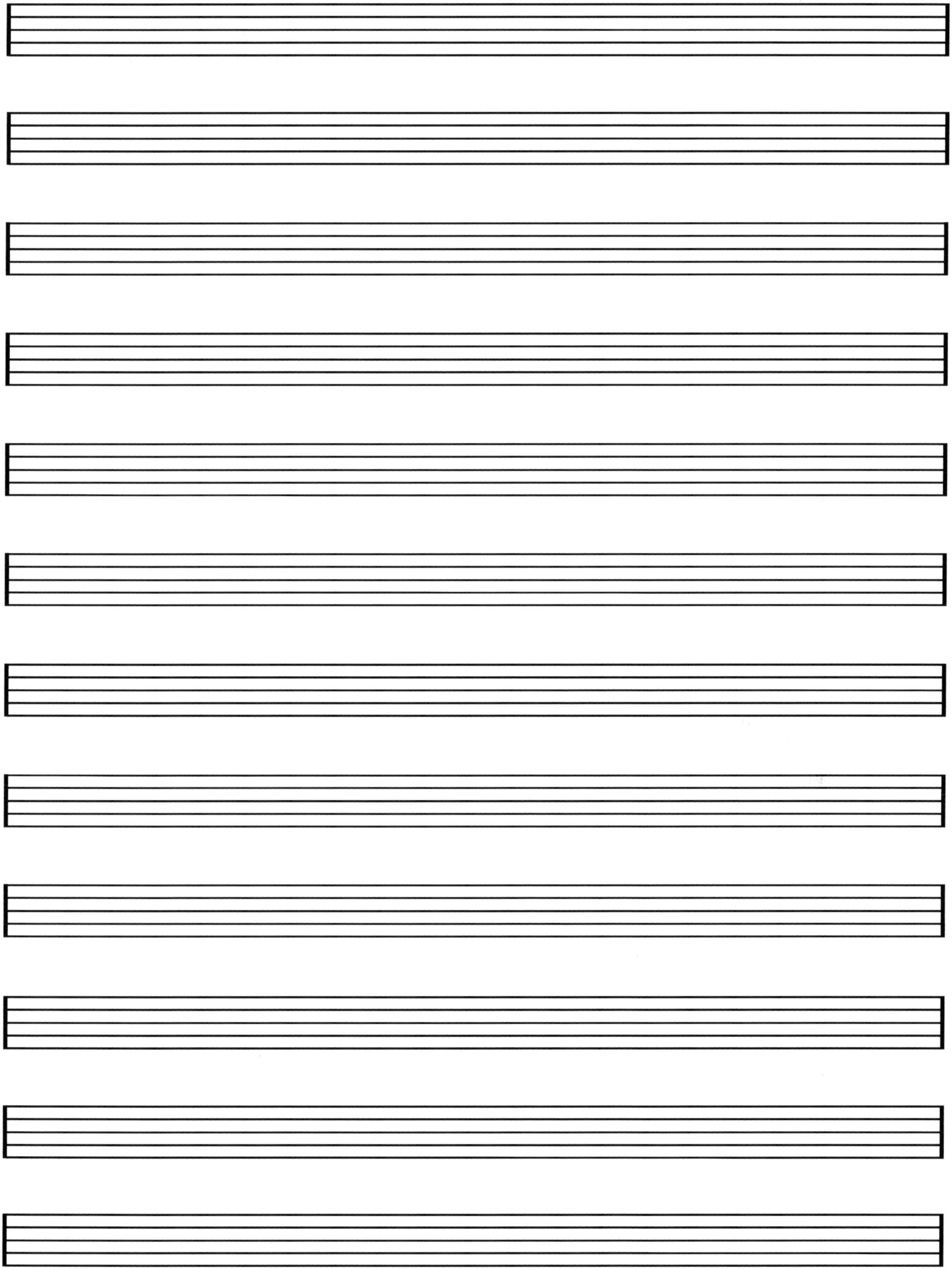

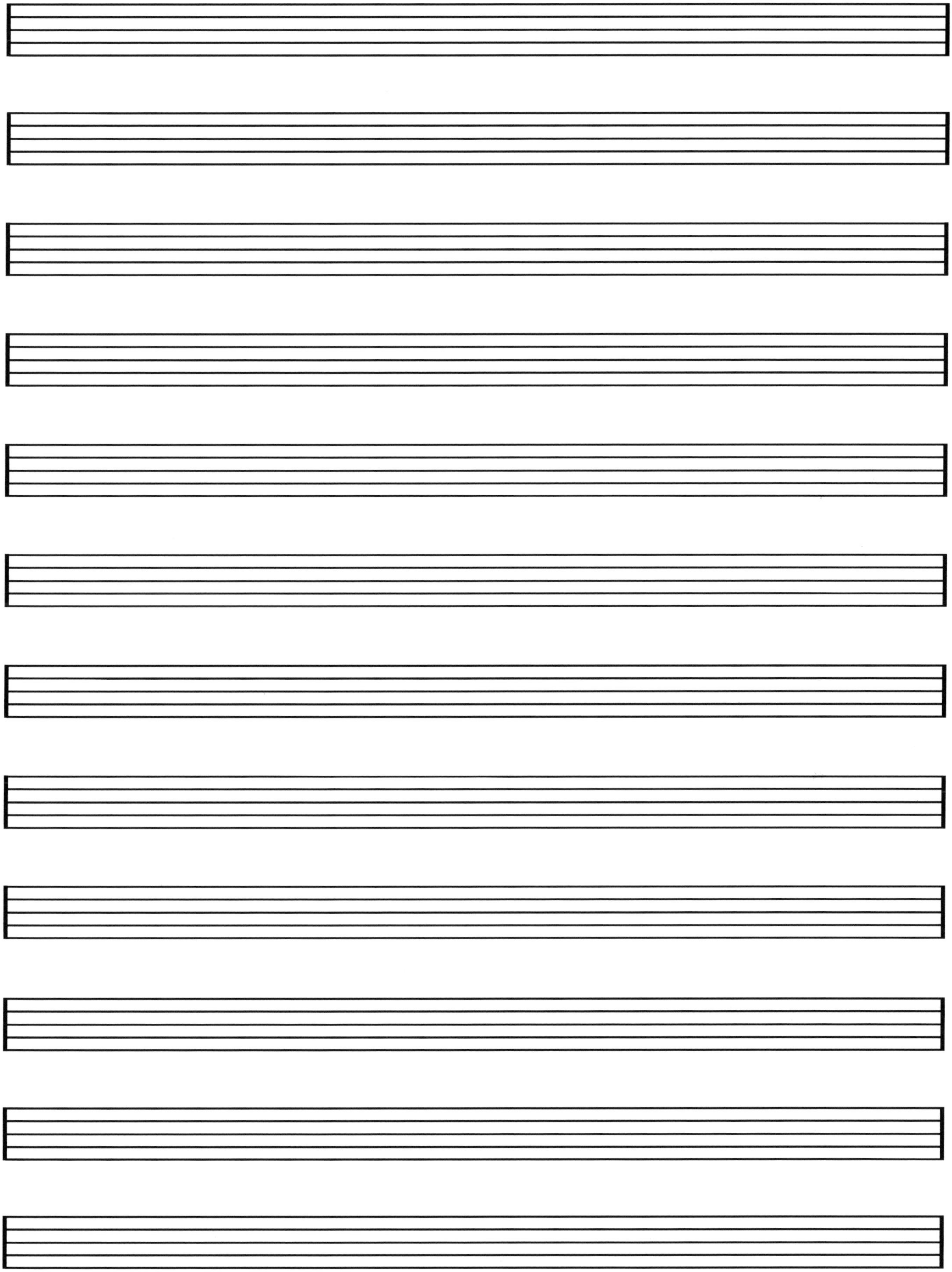

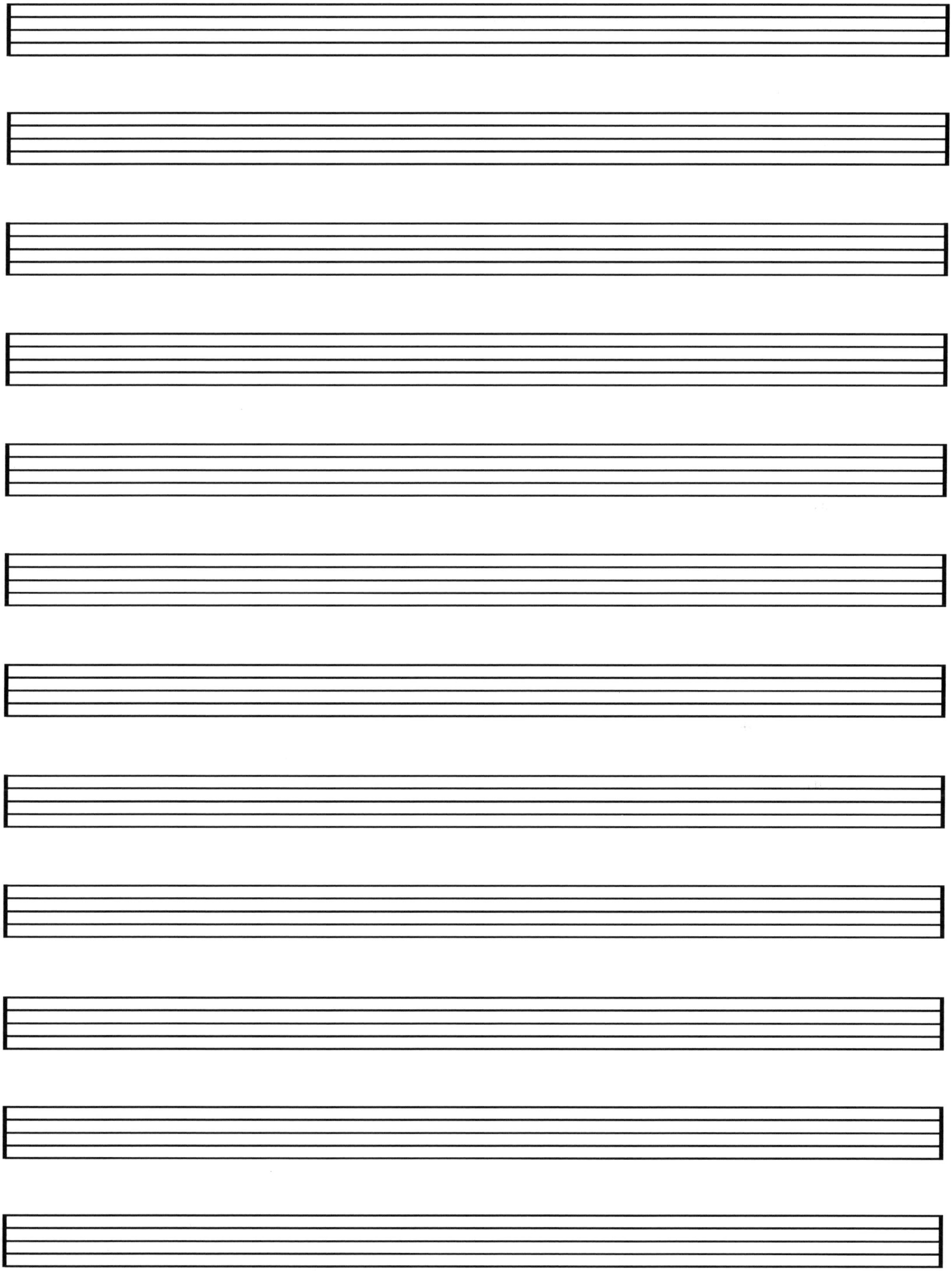

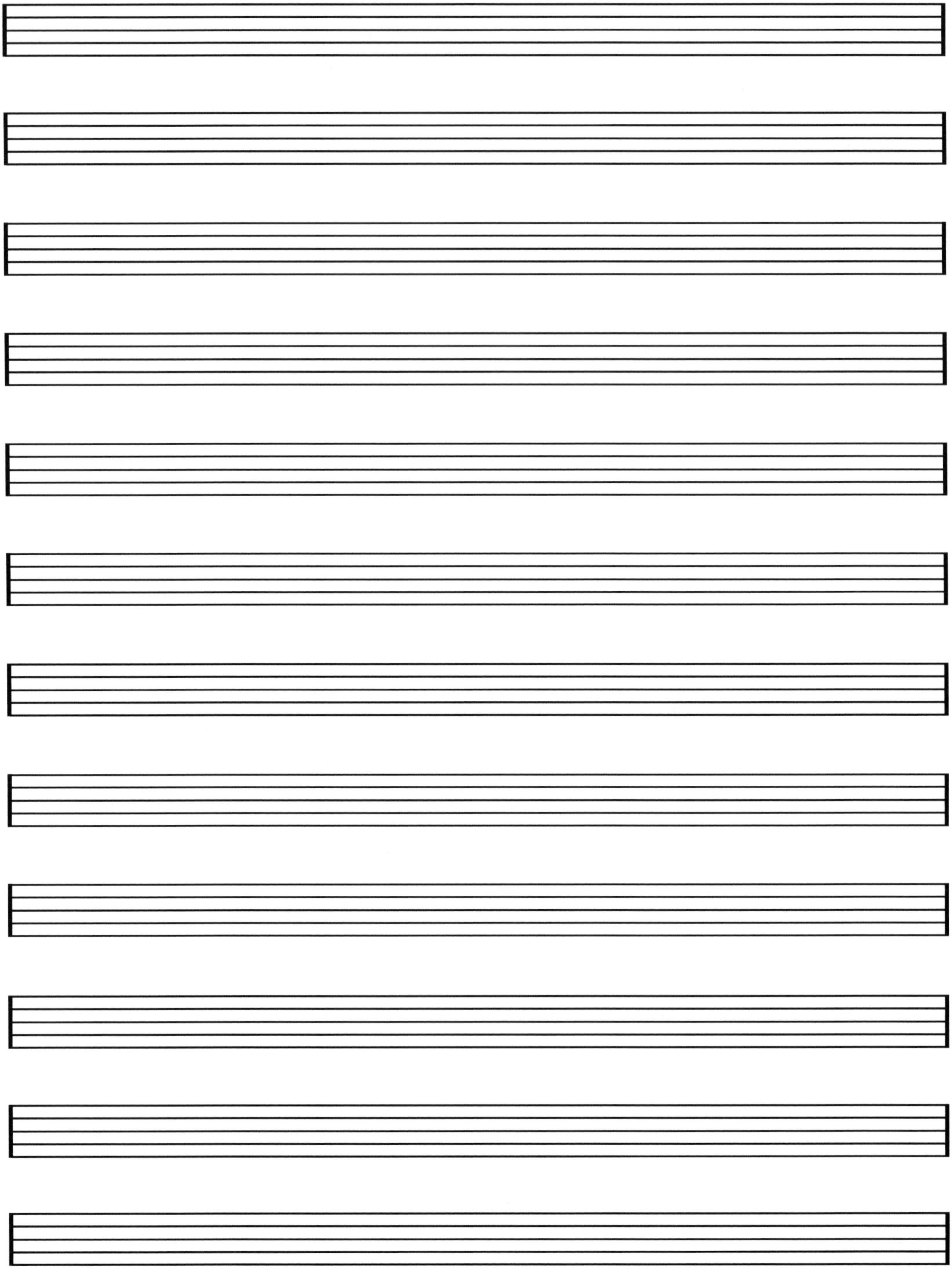

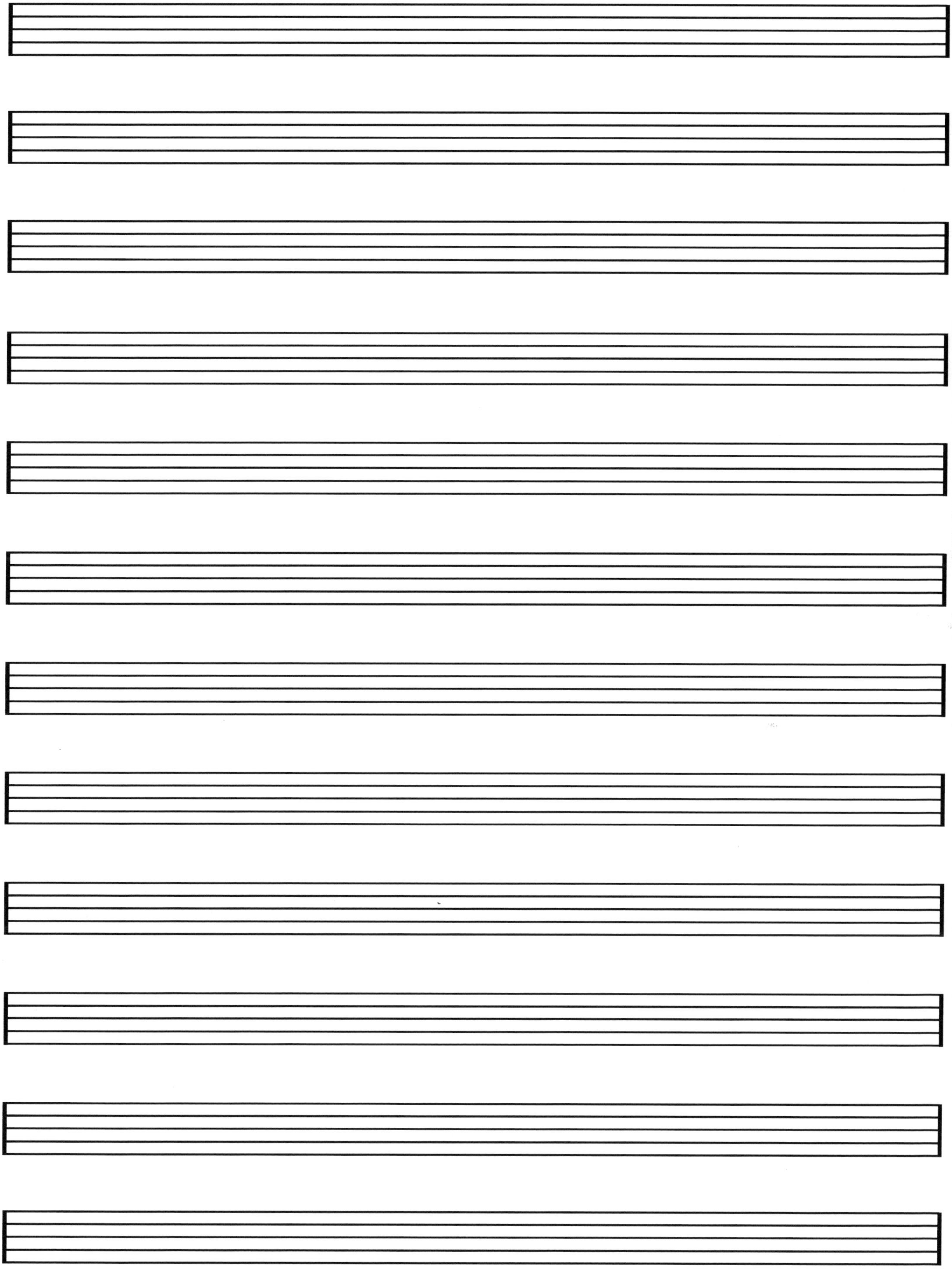

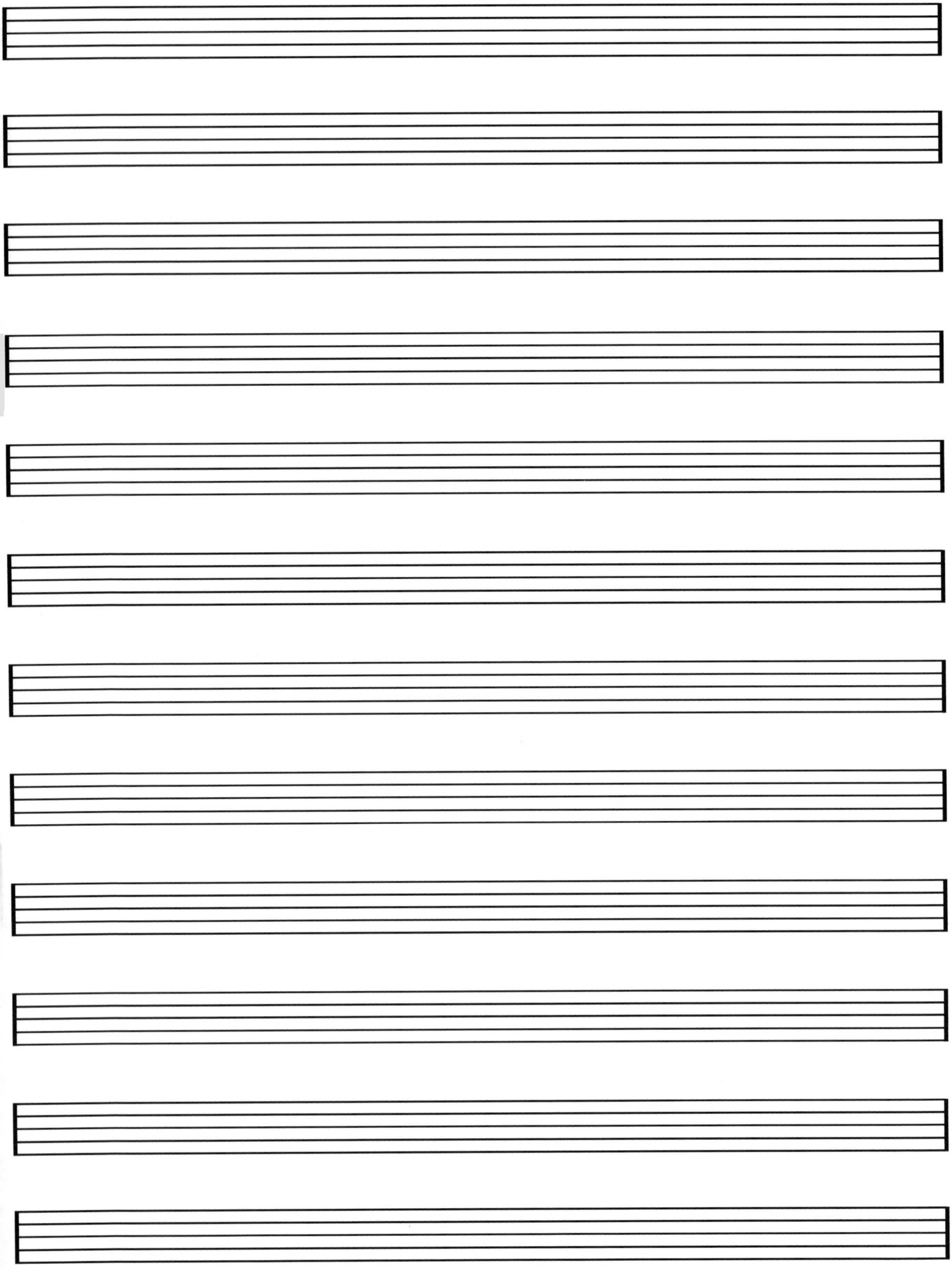

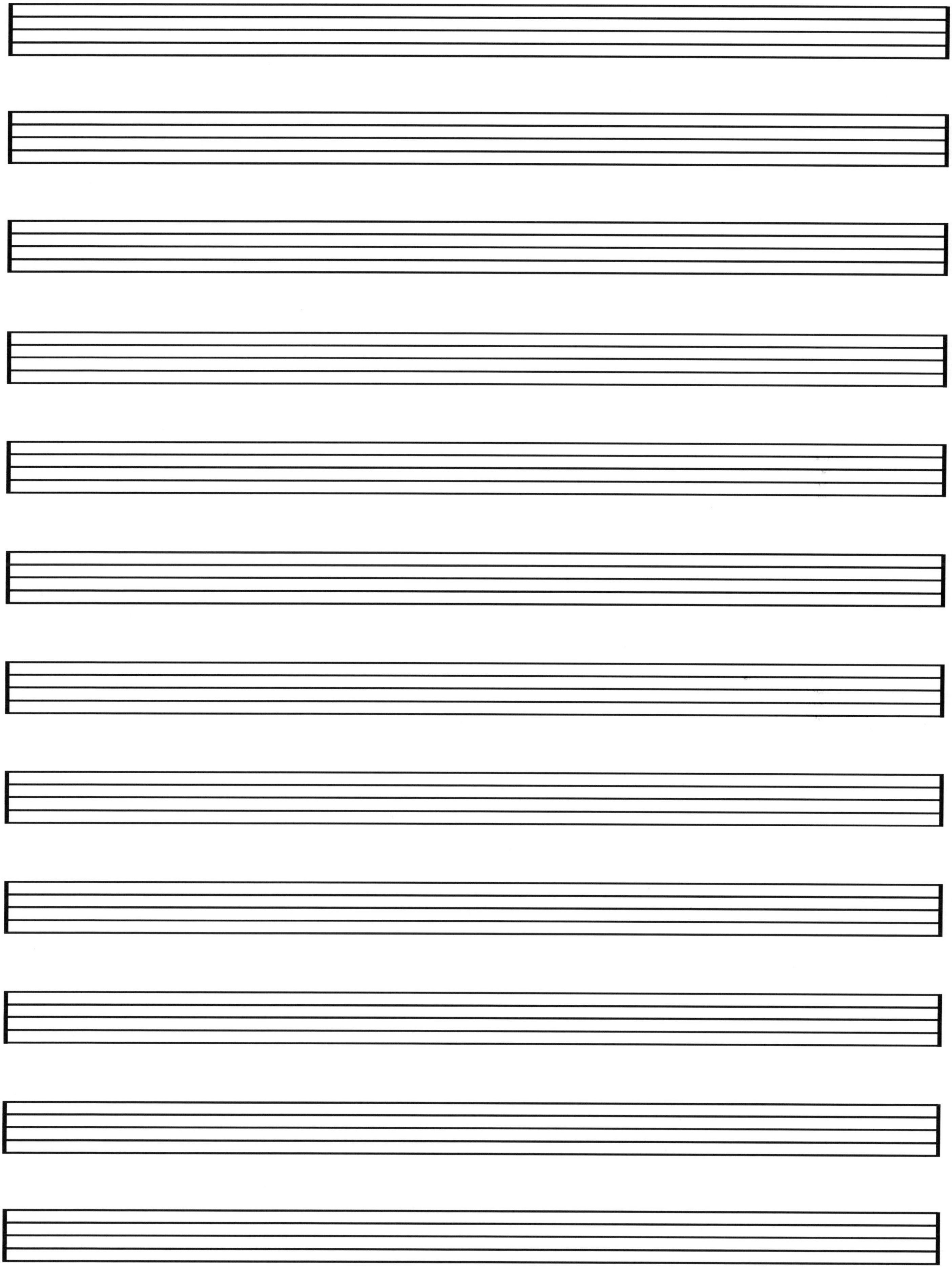

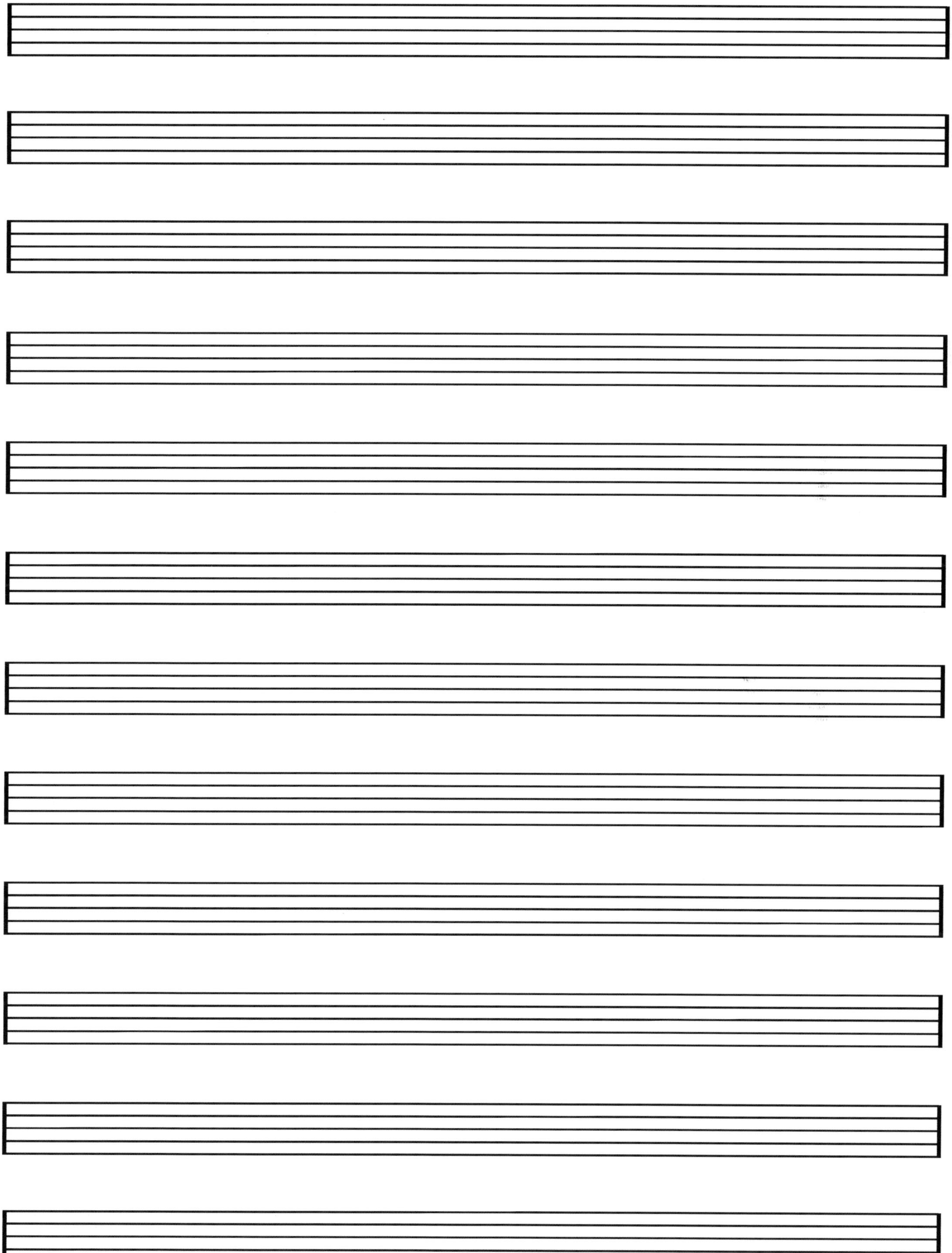

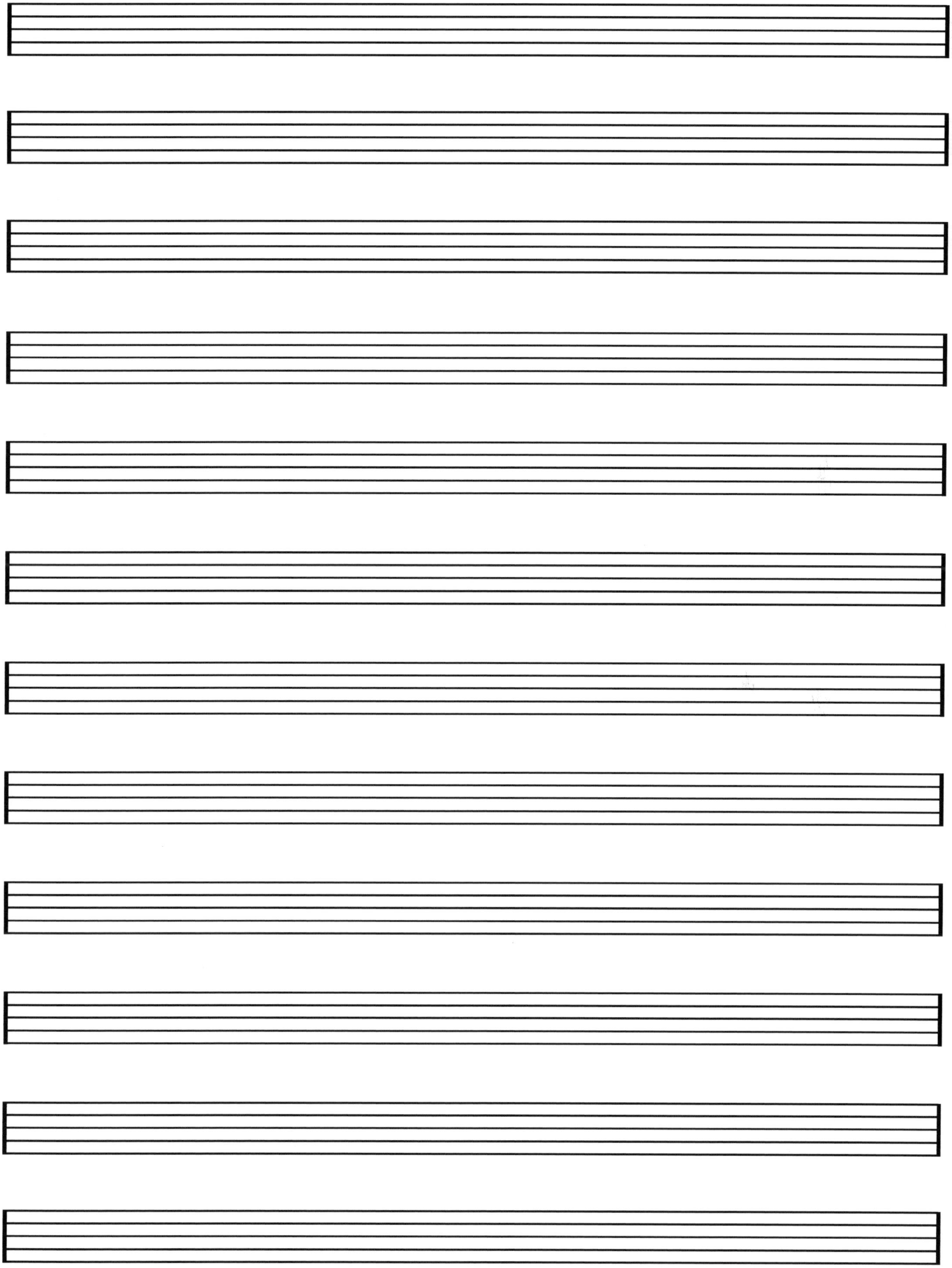

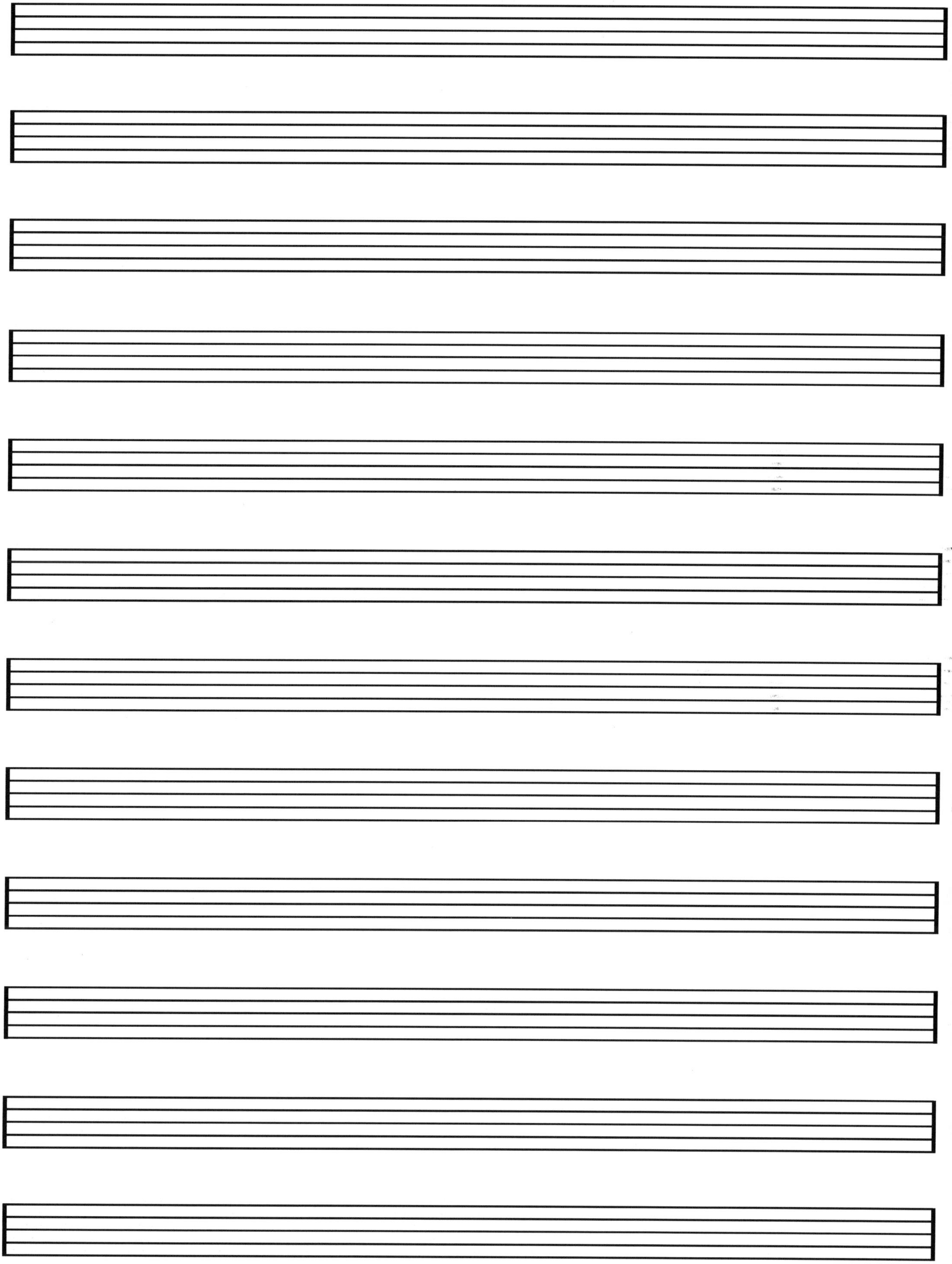

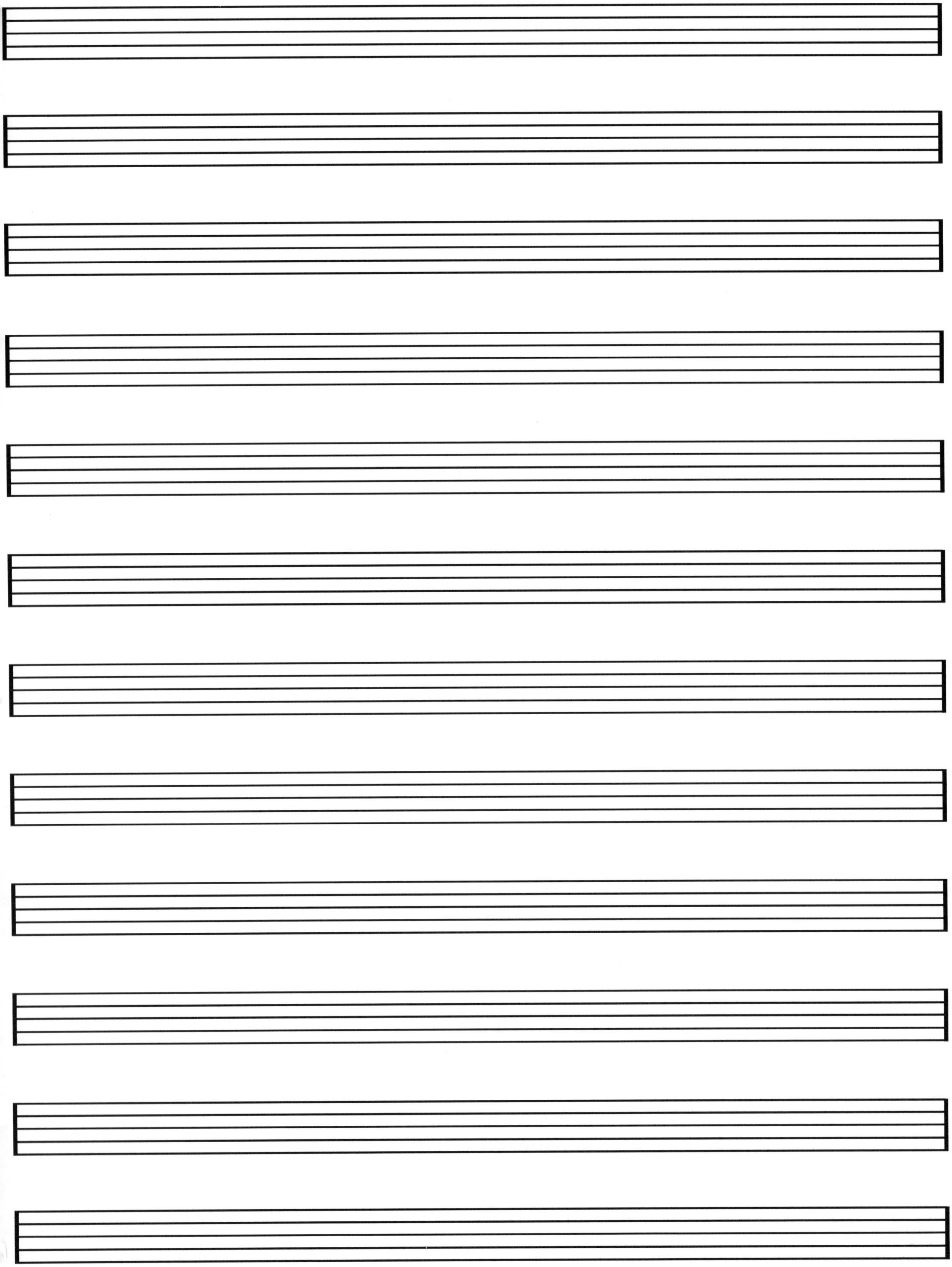

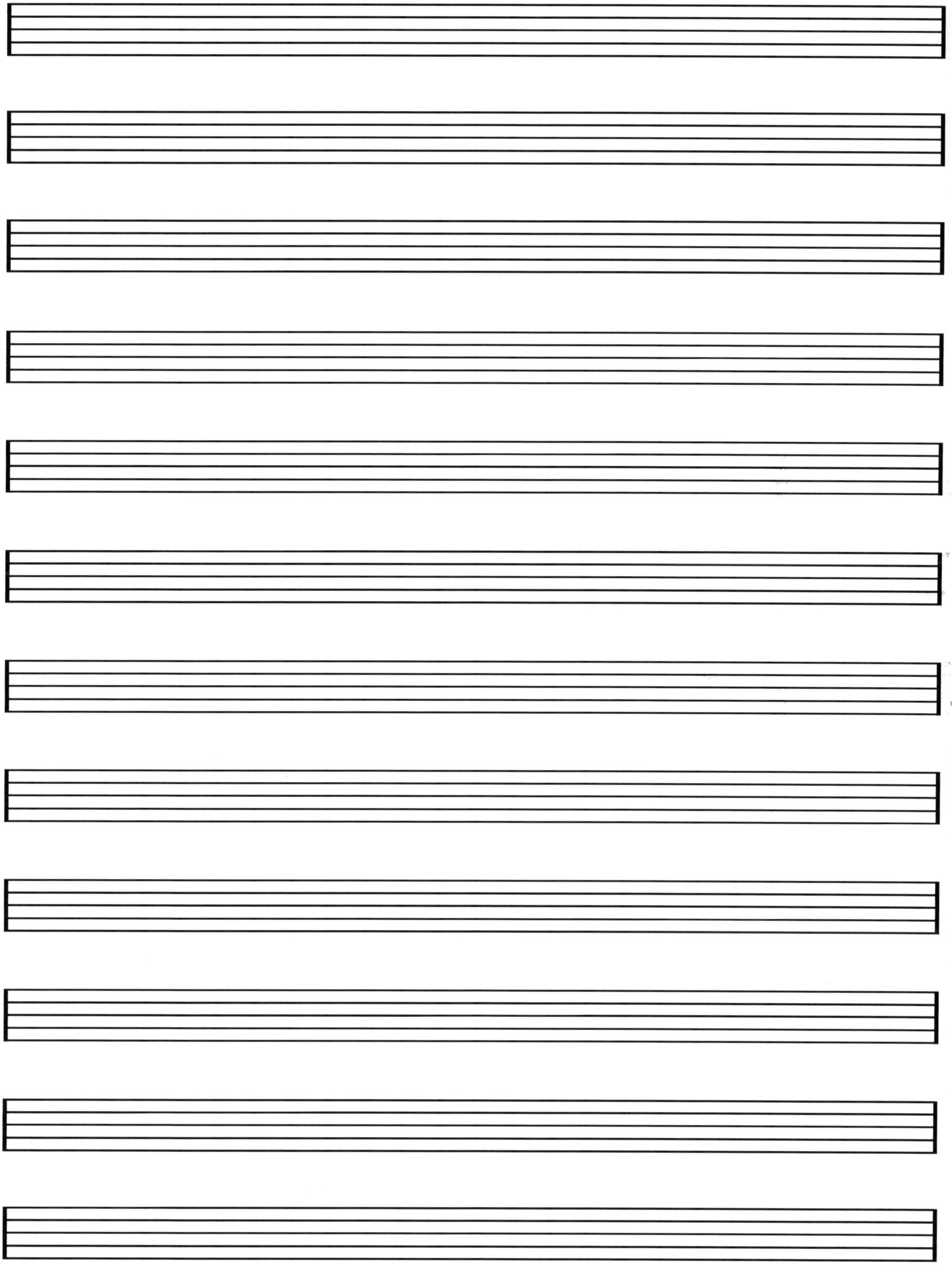

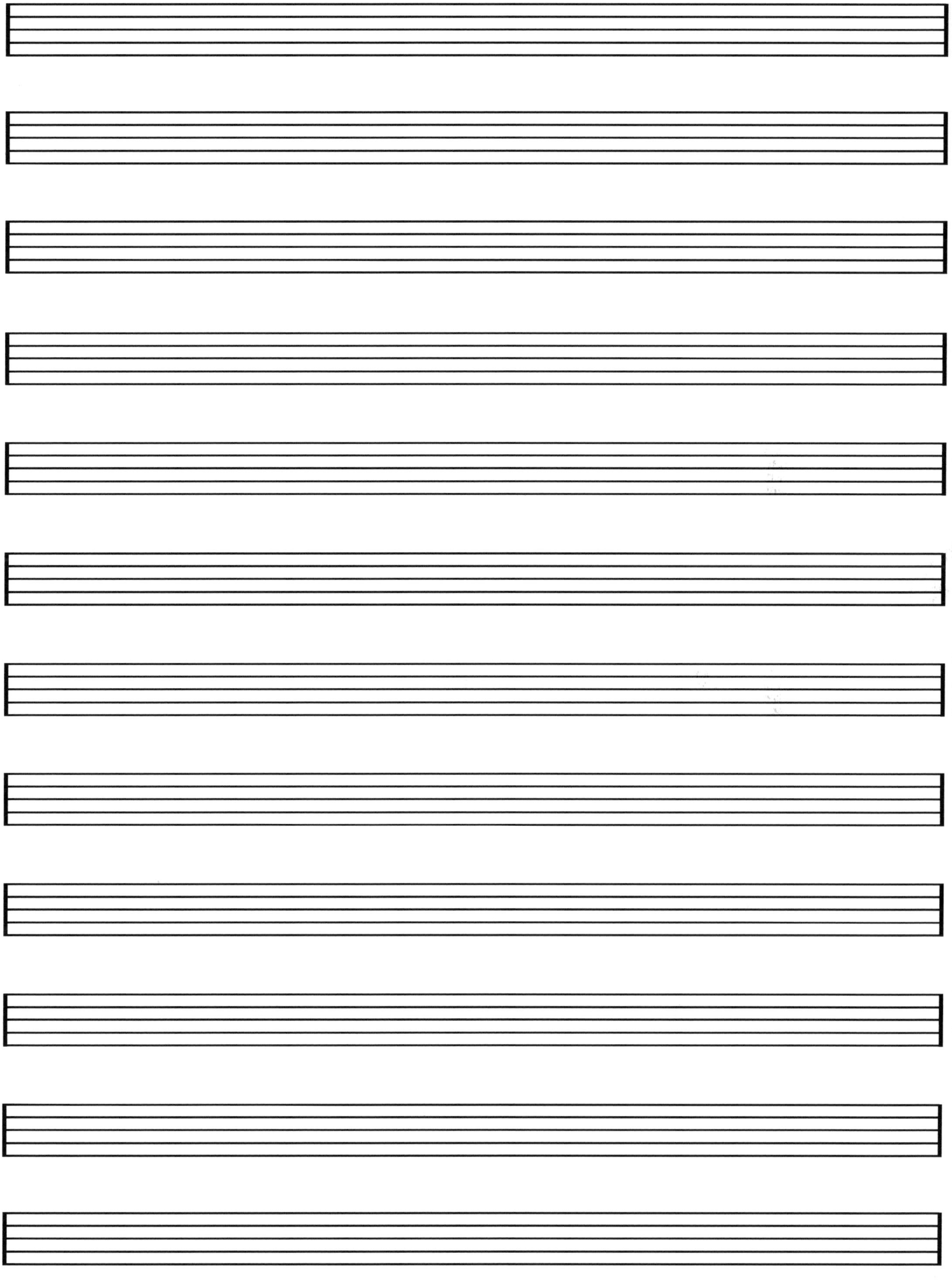

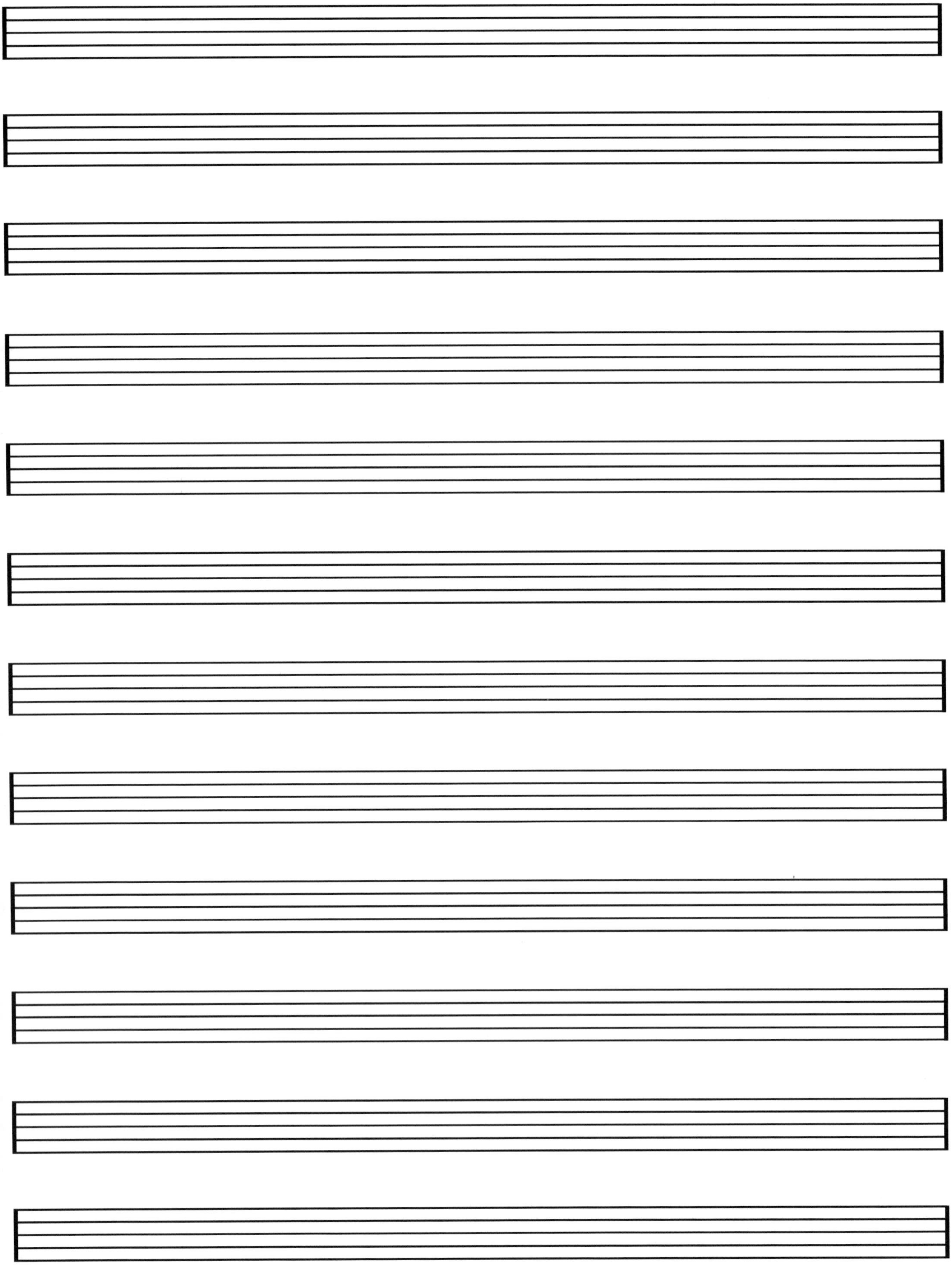

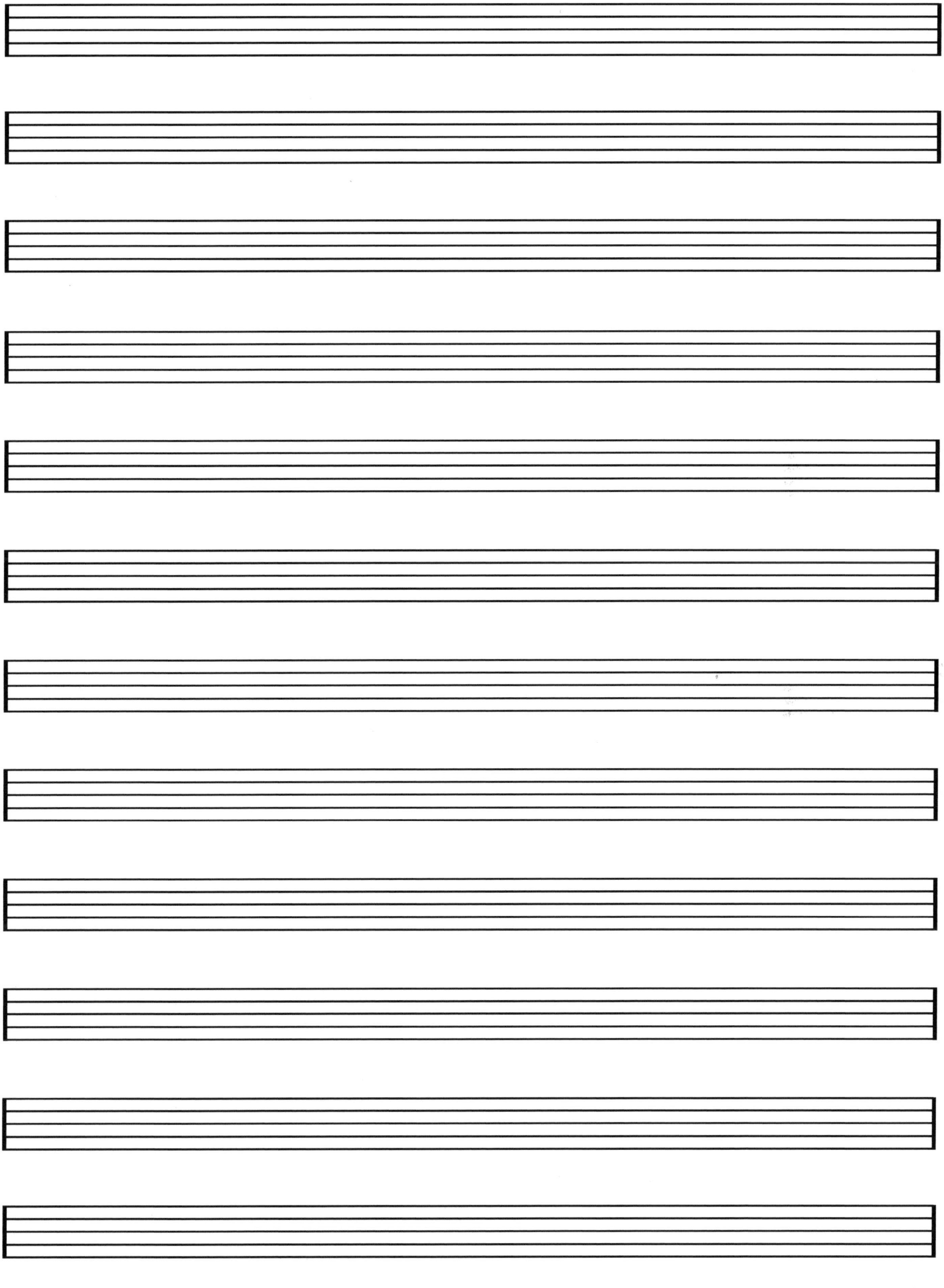

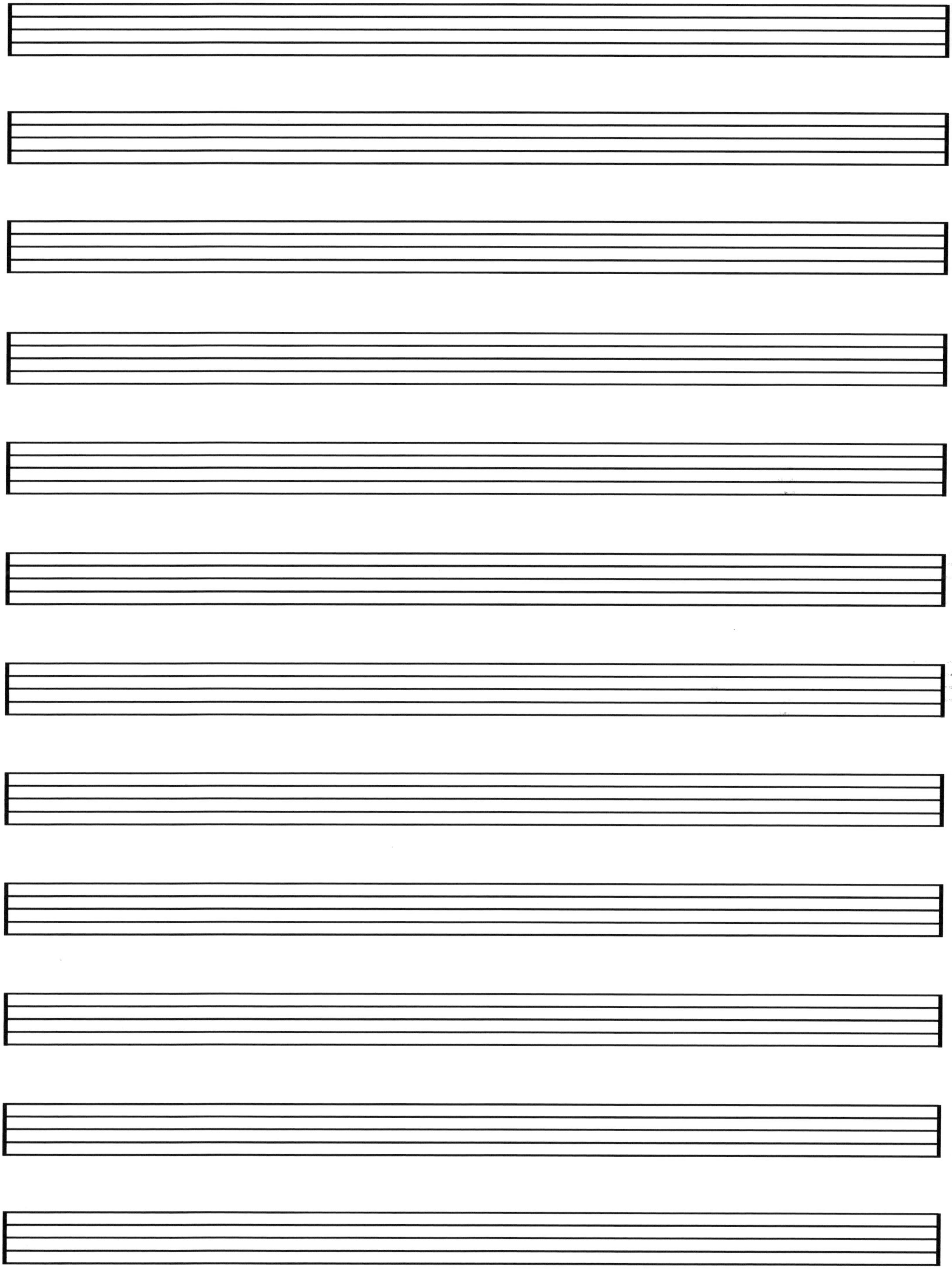

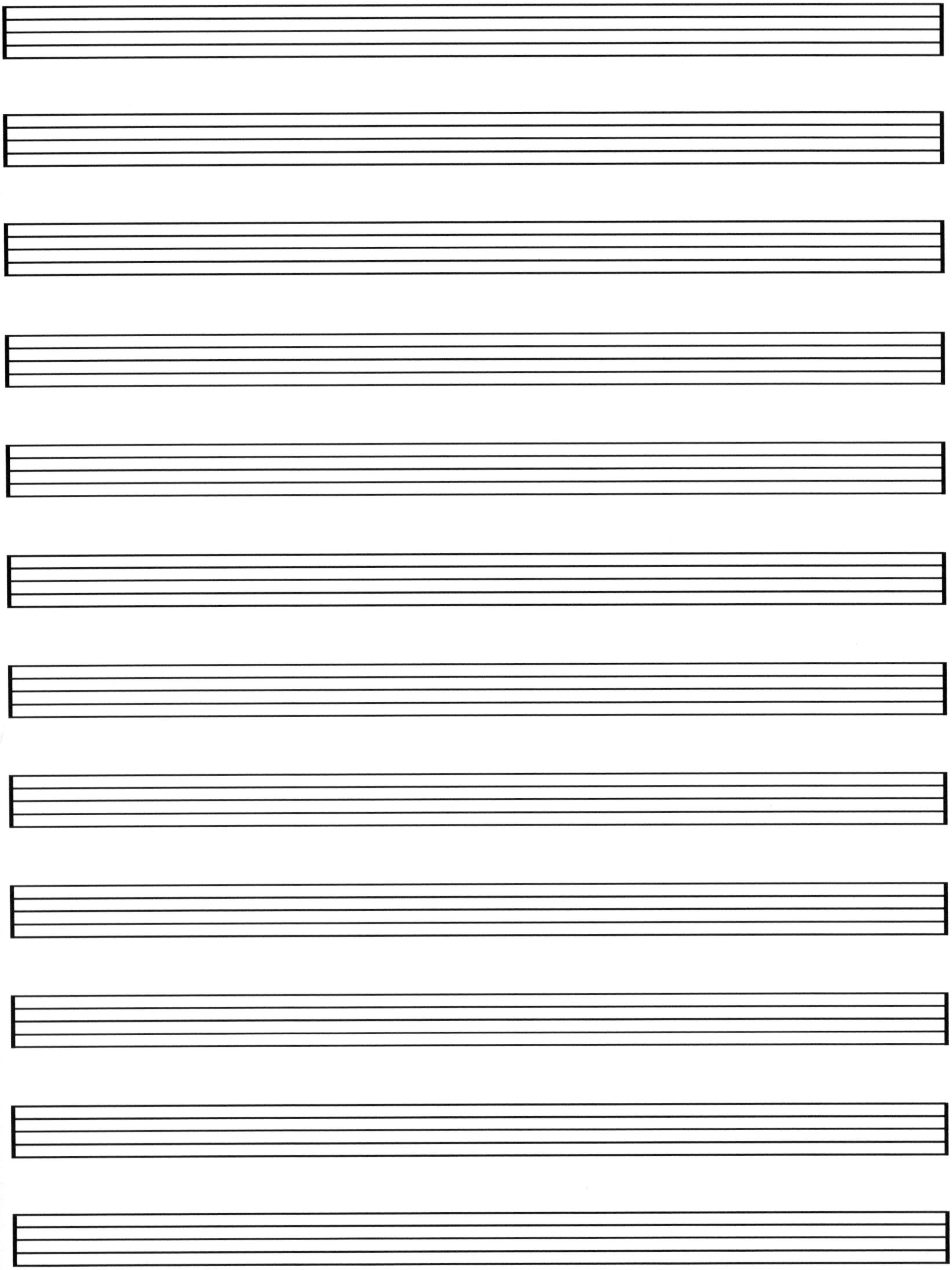

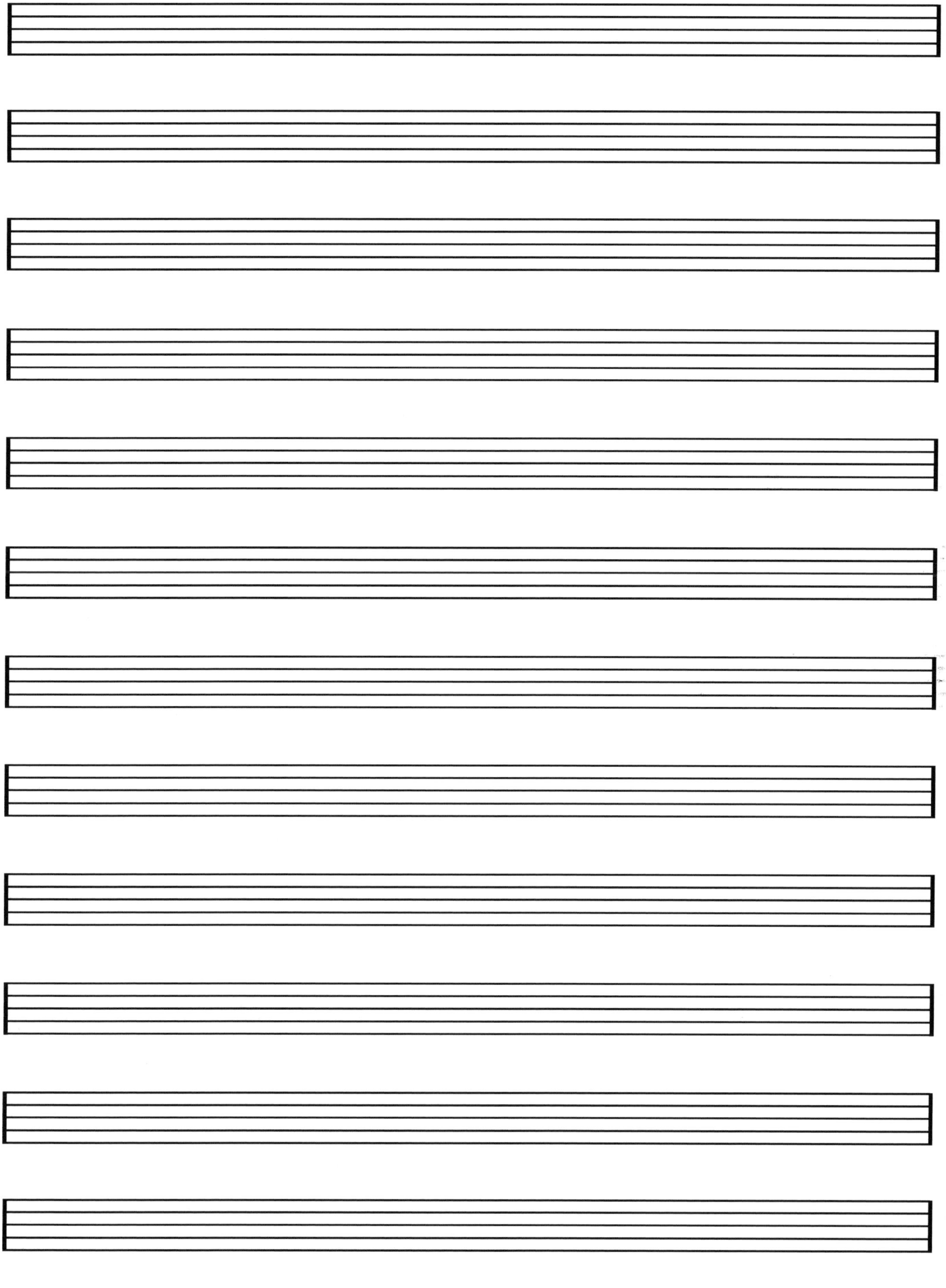

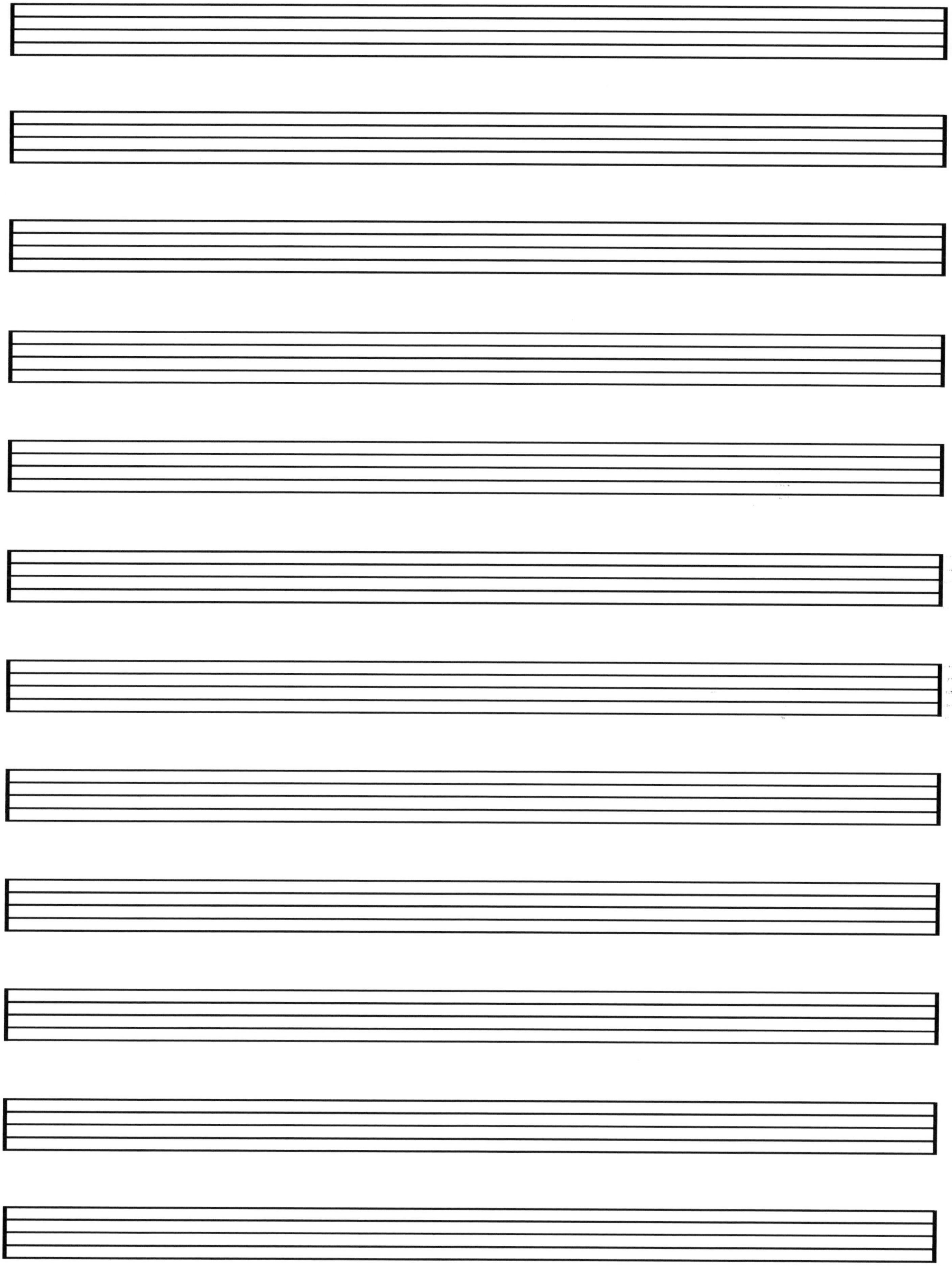

You are great Musician!

Made in the USA
Columbia, SC
16 May 2022

60502921R00057